Stonehenge

Stonehenge

Other titles in the *History's Great Structures* series include:

History's Great
STRUCTURES

Stonehenge

Stephen Currie

ReferencePoint
Press®

San Diego, CA

© 2015 ReferencePoint Press, Inc.
Printed in the United States

For more information, contact:
ReferencePoint Press, Inc.
PO Box 27779
San Diego, CA 92198
www.ReferencePointPress.com

LIBRARY OF CONGRESS CATALOGING-IN-PUBLICATION DATA

Currie, Stephen, 1960-
  Stonehenge / by Stephen Currie.
     pages cm. -- (History's great structures)
  Includes bibliographical references and index.
     ISBN 978-1-60152-712-7 (hardback) -- ISBN 1-60152-712-8 (hardback)
1. Stonehenge (England) 2. Wiltshire (England)--Antiquities. 3. Megalithic monuments--England--Wiltshire. I. Title.
  DA142.C85   2015
  936.2'319--dc23
                                                                    2014010452

CONTENTS

IMPORTANT EVENTS IN THE HISTORY OF STONEHENGE

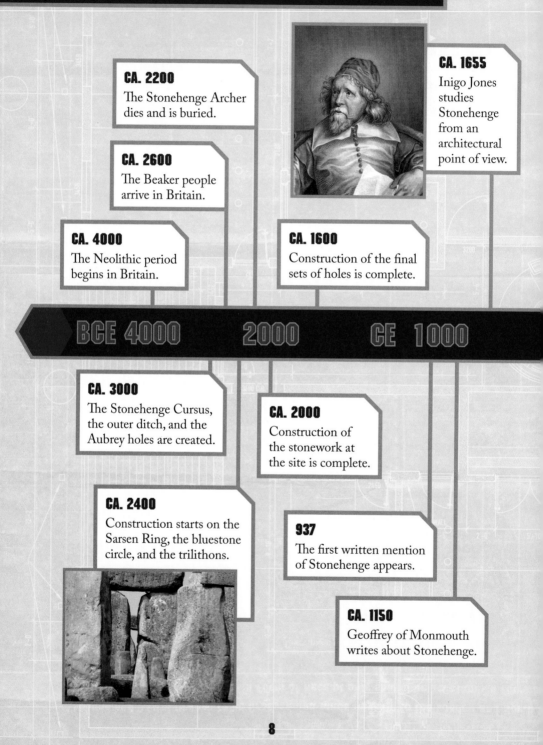

CA. 2200
The Stonehenge Archer dies and is buried.

CA. 1655
Inigo Jones studies Stonehenge from an architectural point of view.

CA. 2600
The Beaker people arrive in Britain.

CA. 4000
The Neolithic period begins in Britain.

CA. 1600
Construction of the final sets of holes is complete.

BCE 4000   **2000**   **CE 1000**

CA. 3000
The Stonehenge Cursus, the outer ditch, and the Aubrey holes are created.

CA. 2000
Construction of the stonework at the site is complete.

CA. 2400
Construction starts on the Sarsen Ring, the bluestone circle, and the trilithons.

937
The first written mention of Stonehenge appears.

CA. 1150
Geoffrey of Monmouth writes about Stonehenge.

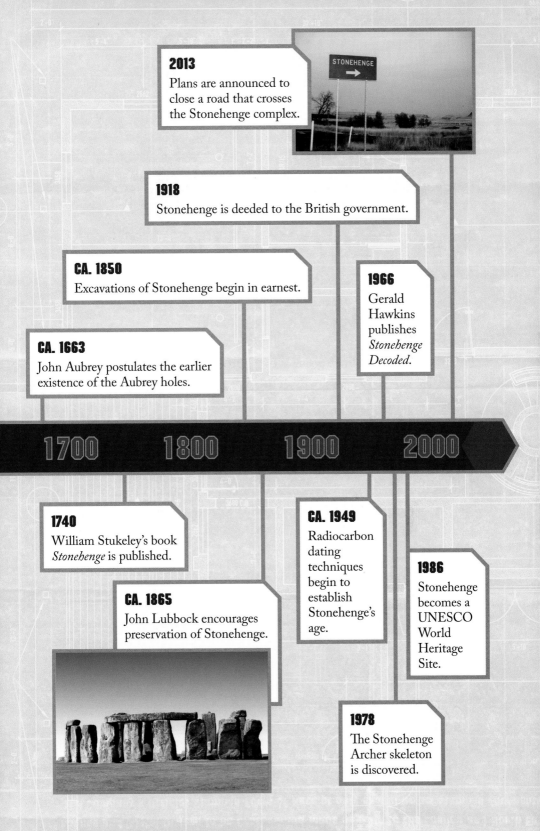

2013
Plans are announced to close a road that crosses the Stonehenge complex.

1918
Stonehenge is deeded to the British government.

CA. 1850
Excavations of Stonehenge begin in earnest.

1966
Gerald Hawkins publishes *Stonehenge Decoded*.

CA. 1663
John Aubrey postulates the earlier existence of the Aubrey holes.

1700   1800   1900   2000

1740
William Stukeley's book *Stonehenge* is published.

CA. 1949
Radiocarbon dating techniques begin to establish Stonehenge's age.

1986
Stonehenge becomes a UNESCO World Heritage Site.

CA. 1865
John Lubbock encourages preservation of Stonehenge.

1978
The Stonehenge Archer skeleton is discovered.

Stonehenge and the World Around It

Along with the Great Wall of China, the Great Pyramid of Giza, and a handful of other buildings, Stonehenge is one of a select few ancient structures recognizable to millions of people worldwide. But while the uses of Egypt's pyramids or China's Great Wall are relatively clear today—the pyramids served mainly as burial chambers, the wall as a means of keeping enemy armies out of Chinese territory—the purpose of the Stonehenge complex is far from clear. Until quite recently, moreover, there was little consensus on who built the structure. Even the question of how it was put together has been difficult to answer precisely. Stonehenge, then, is not merely among the most famous of ancient structures; it is also among the world's least understood and most enigmatic examples of prehistoric architecture.

Located in the Salisbury Plain section of southern England, Stonehenge is not so much a building as a complex. It is best known today for a large stone circle, which consist largely of two parts: uprights, which are embedded in the ground and soar up into the sky; and lintels, horizontal blocks of stone that sit on top of the uprights and are connected to one another. Today, many of the stones have vanished or been damaged, but the original arrangement can easily be deduced by looking at those that remain in position. The stones have intrigued millions of visitors over the years, many of whom have found the scene nearly magical. "Even the most indifferent passenger over the plain must be attracted by the solitary and magnificent appearance of these ruins," wrote Richard Colt Hoare, a Stonehenge expert of the early 1800s, "and all with one accord will exclaim, 'HOW GRAND! HOW WONDERFUL! HOW INCOMPREHENSIBLE!'"[1]

Though the stones are the most striking feature of Stonehenge, they are not the only part of the Stonehenge complex, and from an archeological perspective, they may not even be the most interesting part. Within the stone circle—and in some cases outside it—appear dozens of small holes at regular intervals, many though not all of them forming circles of their own. A long ditch surrounds the stones, and causeways lead across the ditch and into the central monument area. Earthworks called barrows sit here and there at the outskirts of the site. Finally, the site includes a handful of single, isolated stones placed at intervals around the complex. The function of most of these features is not much better understood than the function of the stone circle.

> **WORDS IN CONTEXT**
> consensus
> *Agreement.*

Theories and Speculation

Over the years the mysteries of Stonehenge have intrigued a succession of scholars, thinkers, and ordinary people. Written records discussing Stonehenge go back to the Middle Ages, and even then these English observers were wondering how the monument came to be. According to Henry of Huntingdon, a writer of the 1100s, the problem was perplexing indeed. "No one can conceive how such great stones have been so raised aloft," he noted, "or why they were built there."[2] Others of the same time period seemed less confused by the site, however. They understood the mysteries of Stonehenge, or at least they claimed to understand them. Geoffrey of Monmouth, another writer of the 1100s, stated firmly that Stonehenge was the final resting place of Uther Pendragon, the father of Britain's legendary King Arthur, and that the complex had been constructed largely by Arthur's assistant, the wizard Merlin. There was no evidence to

Among the least understood and most enigmatic examples of prehistoric architecture, Stonehenge continues to fascinate people around the world. Many of the stones have disappeared over time, but enough of the structure remains to give visitors an idea of how it might have looked long ago.

support either of these claims; then again, there was no evidence to disprove them either, and the question of Stonehenge's purpose and construction remained open for debate.

Since medieval times speculation about Stonehenge has only increased. As early as 1695 an Englishman named Edmund Gibson noted that "almost every one has advanced a new notion"[3] about the origin and meaning of Stonehenge. Some have called Stonehenge the work of Stone Age peoples, others the brainchild of Roman-era priests, still others the product of wandering people from Phoenicia in the Middle East; people have claimed that Stonehenge is primarily a hospital, a stadium, a temple, and much more. The modern history of Stonehenge is in many ways the story of the conflict between groups seeking to interpret Stonehenge in ways that make sense to them—whether the evidence supports that interpretation or not.

As of 2014, advanced archeological techniques have allowed researchers to learn a great deal about Stonehenge. Their work has settled some important questions. It is now clear, for instance, that the site was built in stages rather than all at once, and that the beginning and the end of the project were separated by fifteen hundred years or more. Research has also helped provide insight into the function of the site, though conclusions about how the site was used are considerably less certain than conclusions about when it was built. Likewise, although there is plenty of disagreement about how Stonehenge was constructed, recent studies have helped eliminate some earlier theories. In any case, even as scientific understanding and techniques continue to progress, the modern-day understanding of Stonehenge is still evolving.

Today, whether drawn to the site for spiritual or archeological reasons, whether motivated by the desire to see one of the world's oldest existing structures, or by the fun of trying to puzzle out the motivations for building it in the first place, Stonehenge ranks as one of the more popular tourist destinations in Great Britain—and beyond. More than a million visitors come to the site each year, a figure that includes tens of thousands who arrive at Stonehenge to celebrate the summer solstice in late June. Seven of every ten visitors, moreover, come from outside the United Kingdom, making Stonehenge an extremely popular destination for international visitors. Though the monument is neither large nor especially imposing, and though it is in far from perfect shape, its uniqueness and mystery continue to speak to visitors in a myriad of ways. Few sites anywhere on Earth are more compelling.

CHAPTER ONE

The Site

According to the best estimates of archeologists, Stonehenge was completed around 1600 BCE. One of the few certainties about the site is that it no longer looks as it did when it was finished. Indeed, that has been the case for at least the last thousand years and probably much longer. Wind, rain, wildlife, and human activities have all damaged every part of the site over time. While the changes have been in most ways extensive—less than half the original stonework remains in place, for example, and by far the largest share of the holes from the original construction have been filled in—archeologists nevertheless have a clear idea of how the site looked at various points during the process.

The Sarsen Ring

The large stone circle at Stonehenge is sometimes known as the Sarsen Circle or the Sarsen Ring, named after the type of stones the builders used to construct it. Sarsen is a very hard type of sandstone. Indeed, because of sarsen's strength and toughness, it is often used even today as a substitute for concrete in making outdoor steps, curbs, and similar objects. The ancient builders of Stonehenge no doubt recognized the value of building the uprights with such strong materials. In addition to strength, sarsen had a second advantage: It was easy to find in the immediate region. Because the blocks of sarsen occur naturally in the area, it was feasible, if not exactly easy, to transport the blocks to the Stonehenge complex.

Today many of the stones of the Sarsen Ring have disappeared, thanks to repurposing, vandalism, and other factors, but enough remain to give visitors a clear sense of how the feature originally looked. The Sarsen Circle was about 108 feet (33 m) in diameter—in modern terms, it covers about a third of a standard soccer field. Thirty of these stones, also called standing stones or uprights, were set vertically. One end of each standing stone was placed in a pit designed to stabilize it, while the other end rose up into the air. The uprights were enormous, with most of them cut so that they measured about 13 feet (4 m) high and 7 feet (2 m) wide; they weighed on average approximately 25 tons (50,000 pounds). The uprights that survive today fit these dimensions more or less exactly.

Other stones were set on top of the standing stones. Each of these rested on a pair of uprights, forming a ring some distance above the ground. These horizontal pieces, known as lintels, were large, though not nearly as massive as the uprights. Though they were not much shorter than the vertical stones, measuring about 10 or 11 feet (3 or 3.5 m) in length, they were considerably thinner and weighed substantially less. Indeed, the

lintels weighed just five tons (10,000 pounds) on average, about a fifth of the weight of the typical standing stone. The lintels sat on top of the uprights, each lintel balanced on two of the standing stones. The lintels were curved slightly on both the inside and the outside to form a genuine circle, not simply a thirty-sided polygon. Although the builders of the stone circle used a sophisticated interlocking method to connect these horizontal giants to one another and to the uprights, the years have been particularly unkind to the lintels; today, just six of them remain in place.

Some of the stones still standing in the Sarsen circle include carvings as well. After years of weathering, many of these carvings are difficult to make out at this point. A few, in fact, are visible only at certain times of the day, when the sunlight strikes them at a particular angle, and others are no longer visible at all; their existence can be

The massive standing stones, or uprights, each weigh about twenty-five tons. The horizontal pieces, or lintels, are considerably thinner and lighter.

determined only by sensitive laser equipment. As of 2012 over 130 carvings have been located on the existing stones; no one knows, of course, how many carvings there may have been on the stones that are no longer present at the site or how many have disappeared entirely without leaving any trace. The carvings show mainly axe heads and daggers, and there are enough of them that one reporter has called Stonehenge a "prehistoric art gallery."[4]

Circles and Horseshoes

The Sarsen Ring is still the most emblematic aspect of Stonehenge, but it is not the only stone arrangement within the monument. Indeed, a second stone ring was constructed directly inside the Sarsen Circle. This inner ring was quite different from the outer circle in several important ways. For one, it was smaller. The diameter of this circle was only about 75 feet (23 m), and the stones that served as the uprights were much shorter than those of the outer circle. Most of these stones were less than 7 feet (2 m) tall, making them only about half the height of the stones in the Sarsen Ring, and they were correspondingly thinner and lighter as well. This circle of stones was also distinctive because it included no lintels. Of the sixty or so stones in the original arrangement, only a few survive today.

Unlike the stones in the outer circle, moreover, the stones that make up the inner ring are not sarsen. Instead, they are a kind of rock known locally as bluestone—a term that encompasses a variety of rocks, the most prominent of which is a material called dolerite. The ring of bluestones, in turn, surrounded yet another arrangement of stones, this one roughly in the shape of a horseshoe. This horseshoe consisted of five separate structures known as trilithons, a word of Greek origin that literally means *three stones*. Each trilithon was made up of two uprights and one lintel, creating a structure that has been likened to a croquet wicket or the lower body of a giant.

In some ways the arrangement of the stones in the horseshoe was much like the arrangement of the outer circle, but the five pieces of the horseshoe stood alone; they were not connected to one another with lintels. Like the outer circle, these stones were sarsen. There the resemblance ended, however, because the sarsen blocks of the horseshoe were much bigger than the sarsen blocks that made up the outer ring. The longest of the uprights in the horseshoe, for example, measured 24 feet (7 m). Perhaps in part because of the size of these stones, the horseshoe is among the best preserved features at Stonehenge. Three of the five original trilithons are still intact.

Just as the outer ring of sarsen blocks surrounded an inner circle made of bluestone, the horseshoe of sarsen trilithons surrounded a group of bluestones as well. And just as the inner bluestone ring consisted of stones that were much smaller than the sarsen stones, the tallest of the bluestone uprights inside the sarsen horseshoe reached

⬡ STONEHENGE IN LITERATURE

Stonehenge has appeared frequently in British literature and occasionally in the literature of other countries as well. That was perhaps especially true in the 1800s and early 1900s. Katharine Lee Bates, best known in the United States for writing "America the Beautiful," wrote a poem called "At Stonehenge" in which she likened the monument to the building blocks of a young giant. "Grim stones whose gray lips keep your secret well," the poem begins, "Our hands that touch you touch an ancient terror." Another poet, William Wordsworth, used Stonehenge as an inspiration for a poem about the power of nature on Salisbury Plain. And the climactic scene of *Tess of the d'Urbervilles*, a late nineteenth century novel by British author Thomas Hardy, takes place in Stonehenge, where the main character spends the night on the Altar Stone.

More recently Stonehenge has become a fixture in novels of fantasy and historical fiction. In 2000 author Bernard Cornwell published a popular novel called *Stonehenge*. The novel, set in 2000 BCE, tells the story of a rivalry between three brothers who live near the monument. British writer Edward Rutherfurd's 1987 novel *Sarum* is another piece of historical fiction; set in Salisbury, the region where Stonehenge is located, it follows the people of the area through many generations and includes the building of Stonehenge among its main events. Stonehenge's majesty and mystery make it likely that it will continue to star in fiction and poetry for many years to come.

Katharine Lee Bates, *The Retinue and Other Poems*. New York: Dutton, 1918, p. 85.

a height of only about 8 feet (2.5 m), considerably shorter than the sarsen uprights that surrounded them. The bluestone horseshoe likewise included no lintels, only uprights. Modern experts believe that there were once nineteen uprights in the bluestone horseshoe. Like other parts of the site, time has taken a significant toll on them. Today, only six of the stones survive.

Other Stones

Though the rings and the horseshoes are the best known arrangements of stones at Stonehenge, the site includes a number of other stones as well. Unlike the stones in the rings and the horseshoes, most of these are set singly or in pairs. The so-called Altar Stone, for example, stood inside the two horseshoe formations, near the very center of the monument. About 16 feet (5 m) long, it most likely stood upright like the standing stones in the outer ring. Today, however, it has been broken into two parts and lies on the ground. Though the Altar Stone is a type of sandstone, it is not sarsen and therefore has a different origin from the sarsen blocks that surround it. Despite the nickname, there is no evidence that the Altar Stone was ever used as an altar. "Its name," writes author Christopher Chippindale, is simply "a modern fancy as to its original purpose."[5]

Other sarsen stones were placed outside the circles. Several of these are particularly important. One set of sarsens, known today as the Station Stones, stood along an imaginary line crossing the center of the Sarsen Ring. Evidence suggests that there were originally four Station Stones and that they were set in pairs. Currently, however, just one stone of each pair survives. In addition, the Heel Stone, another block of sarsen, stood on its own in the northeastern portion of the site; it still stands in that position today, though its impact on a modern viewer is diminished somewhat because a roadway has been built within a few yards of it. Unlike most of the other stones at the site, the Heel Stone is not rectangular. Instead, it is tapered toward the top. Moreover, authors Leon E. Stover and Bruce Kraig note that the Heel Stone is "leaning badly and terribly weathered."[6]

Near the Heel Stone lies perhaps the most impressive of the sarsen stones outside the Sarsen Circle. This one is known as the Slaughter Stone. "Its upper surface, all humps, bumps and hollows . . . gave it this name," writes Chippindale, "as it seemed in the 18th century so obviously suited to catch the blood of victims sacrificed on it."[7] Modern experts dismiss the notion that the stone was actually used in this manner, but the name has nonetheless stuck. Originally one of a set of stones—certainly two and possibly three—the Slaughter Stone is the only one remaining from the group, and though it was once set vertically, like the uprights in the Sarsen Circle, it currently lies flat on the ground. The Slaughter Stone and its companions were among the largest stones anywhere in the complex; the surviving stone measures 21 feet (6.5 m) long and up to 7 feet (2 m) wide.

Earthworks, Ditches, and Causeways

A modern visitor to Stonehenge could be forgiven for believing that the sarsens and bluestones dominating the complex were the only remnants of importance at the site. They are, after all, by a considerable margin the site's most visible features. Though some of the other features of Stonehenge are now difficult or nearly impossible to spot, the site nonetheless includes ditches, causeways, and other structures, many of which predate the stones. These are of more interest to archeologists—scientists who study the cultures of the distant past—than to casual visitors, but anyone who wishes to understand the monument as a whole needs to be aware of these features as well.

One of these features is a circular groove or ditch, about 330 feet (100 m) in diameter, that surrounds the Sarsen Ring. The original width of the ditch was about 20 feet (6 m), and its depth was approximately 5 to 7 feet (1.5 to 2 m). The materials excavated in the process of making the ditch were then piled up to create an embankment on one side of the groove. Over years of neglect, much of the ditch has been filled in with earth, and the embankment has been weathered and eroded until it is much smaller than it originally was; the result is that the top of the embankment now stands only a few feet above the bottom of the ditch. Still, unlike several other features at the Stonehenge complex that have by now almost entirely disappeared, the ditch is clearly visible in pictures of the site.

A second feature of Stonehenge consisted of causeways, a type

The Stonehenge Site

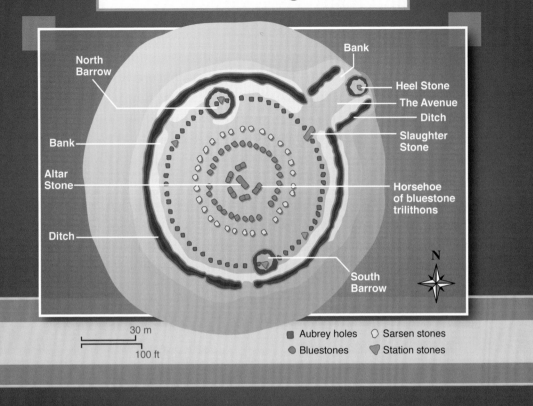

- North Barrow
- Bank
- Bank
- Altar Stone
- Ditch
- Bank
- Heel Stone
- The Avenue
- Ditch
- Slaughter Stone
- Horsehoe of bluestone trilithons
- South Barrow

N

30 m
100 ft

■ Aubrey holes ○ Sarsen stones
● Bluestones ▽ Station stones

Source: Edward Di Cosmo, "The Development of Stonehenge," www.personal.psu.edu.

of low bridge that allowed people to cross the ditch quickly and easily. Archeologists generally believe that there were two causeways, though some evidence suggests that there may once have been three. The biggest causeway was set up in the northeastern part of the site; the Heel Stone, which may possibly date from the same period, was placed in the middle of this causeway. The large causeway was about 35 feet (11 m) wide. In modern times it is known as the Avenue. At the same time, another causeway most likely entered the complex from the south. This one was perhaps less used because it was narrower—only about 13 feet (4 m) in width. Today, the larger causeway still remains easily visible, but the causeway to the south has almost entirely disappeared.

Holes and Pits

Other features of Stonehenge are more difficult for modern tourists to locate. These include a set of pits dug into the ground, known today as the Aubrey holes. When these holes were created they formed a ring slightly smaller than the ditch and with the same center. There were fifty-six of the holes in all, and they were relatively large; the average hole was just over 3 feet (.91 m) in diameter and had a depth of more than 2 feet (0.61 m). For some reason unknown today, however, the holes were filled in soon after they were created. Their existence was not known until the 1600s, when a scholar named John Aubrey identified a few spots that might once have been holes, and their existence was not suspected until the 1920s. Though they did not last long, and though they have left very little trace today, the Aubrey holes were an important feature of Stonehenge when the complex was first constructed.

In addition to the Aubrey holes, Stonehenge was built with a variety of other holes and pits as well. For example, Stonehenge once included a series of postholes. They most likely contained poles made out of timber, but the poles have long since disappeared. These holes were placed in rows along the two causeways that entered the monument. In contrast to the Aubrey holes, the postholes were quite small; they were less than half the diameter of the Aubrey holes and not nearly as deep. Their spacing also seems to have been less regular than the spacing of the Aubrey holes. Like many of the Stonehenge features, the postholes have largely disappeared today, and their existence must be inferred mainly from archeological clues.

WORDS IN CONTEXT

integral
Of central importance.

The ancient creators of Stonehenge also dug other sets of holes at the site. Two of these sets are known today as the Q and R holes. They appeared in the center of the site, just inside the Sarsen Circle. Exactly what these holes looked like is largely a matter of conjecture, as is how they were arranged. They have almost entirely disappeared today, and indeed their existence is known only through careful archeological work. The best evidence, however, indicates that they formed two small circles with perhaps as many as forty holes in each ring. At one point they most likely held stones, probably bluestones, though this again is open to some interpretation. As with many other features of the Stonehenge site, much about the Q and R holes remains unknown today. It is not even certain whether the two circles were ever completed, how many of the holes held bluestones, or when, let alone why, the stones were removed.

Two other sets of holes, known today as the Y and Z holes, were probably among the last features of Stonehenge to be constructed. Like the Q and R holes, the Y and Z holes are no longer visible, and their existence would have remained undetected if not for modern archeological methods. The Y and Z holes are even more mysterious than the other holes at the site. Author Rosemary Hill says that the set of holes "seems never to have served any function."[8] Indeed, as far as archeologists can tell, the holes never contained any objects at all. What their purpose was will likely never be known.

Beyond the Embankment

Besides the structures, holes, and ditches inside the circular ditch and embankment, the Stonehenge site also included several other features lying beyond the embankment. One of these was a long and wide embankment-and-ditch construction known as the Stonehenge Cursus. The word *cursus* comes from the Latin for *racecourse*; originally the cursus was believed to have been built by the Romans and used as a racetrack for chariots, and though the feature turns out to have no connection with the Romans at all, the name has stuck. The Stonehenge cursus ran roughly east-west; it was about 1.8 miles (3 km) long and 110 yards (100 m) wide. Over the years the cursus has been severely damaged by the force of nature and by human activity, notably farming. Today, not much of the cursus is visible.

A second cursus, the Lesser Cursus, also was constructed near the rest of the site. Much smaller than the Stonehenge Cursus, the Lesser

⬡ AVEBURY

Several other prehistoric monuments in Britain have strong similarities to Stonehenge. Chief among these is a site known as Avebury, about 30 miles (48 km) north of Stonehenge. Like Stonehenge, Avebury includes a circular ditch and embankment that encloses a variety of stones set up for purposes that are not clear today. In particular, Avebury includes three concentric stone circles, the outermost of which is the largest stone circle in Europe. Though not as widely investigated by archeologists as Stonehenge, Avebury nonetheless has been proved to date to the same time period as its more famous relative, and indeed the two have been linked together by various historic preservation groups. UNESCO, an organization interested in sites of cultural importance, considers Stonehenge and Avebury to be a single complex for its purposes.

While Avebury resembles Stonehenge in many ways, there are some important differences. The ditch and embankment are more prominent at Avebury than they are at Stonehenge, for instance. On the other hand, the stones at Avebury are typically shorter and spaced more widely apart than those of Stonehenge. Moreover, there are no lintels at Avebury; this omission makes the monument seem lower and less sophisticated than Stonehenge.

The similarities were sufficient, though, to help seventeenth-century researcher John Aubrey understand Stonehenge better. Seeing some holes in the ground at Avebury, he reasoned that some faint depressions at Stonehenge might once have been holes themselves; this was the first indication of what are now known as the Aubrey holes.

Cursus was only about 500 yards (about 457 m) long and was just over half as wide as the Stonehenge Cursus. Like the Stonehenge Cursus, the Lesser Cursus suffered in the years following its construction. Although parts of it remained visible into the 1900s, farming and other activities have very nearly erased it from the Stonehenge landscape altogether. The same has happened to several other monuments in the vicinity of the cursus structures. In particular, a barrow, or earth mound surrounded by a ditch, was at one point located at one end of the Stonehenge Cursus; it has long since been leveled, however.

Finally, the site also included a palisade, or wooden fence, to the northwest of the Sarsen Circle. Like many of the other features of Stonehenge, the fence has vanished with little trace except to the skilled eyes of archeologists aided by increasingly sensitive equipment. And again like many of the rest of the site's features, the purpose of this fence is unclear. Perhaps it was built to keep enemies away—but the fence does not appear to have been long enough or strong enough to serve as much protection. It may instead have had a religious purpose or have been used for some other reason no one has yet been able to determine. Like much else at the Stonehenge site, there are more mysteries surrounding the palisade than there are answers.

The standard picture of Stonehenge is of a large stone circle, damaged by humans and weather over the years but still sufficiently intact to awe and inspire. That stone circle is certainly a part of Stonehenge, but it is by no means the only part. In addition to the famous circle of sarsen stones, Stonehenge also includes a variety of other stones, some still standing, and a large number of holes, ditches, causeways, and other features. Though most of these features have not held up well, and though many of them have disappeared more or less completely through the centuries since they were originally constructed, they were nevertheless deemed important by the people who built the site. Given the time and energy it would have taken to construct them, it is fair to say that they were as integral a part of the monument as the rings of sarsen and bluestone.

CHAPTER TWO

The Builders

Stonehenge was built not just over a period of many years but a period of many generations. The most recent scholarship regarding the monument suggests that approximately fifteen hundred years passed between the time construction began and the time it was finished. In modern terms, that is as if a project had been started at the beginning of the medieval period in about 600 CE and was not completed until the end of the twentieth century. Even granted that society changed much more slowly in prehistoric times than it does today, that still means that people from many different cultures worked on the site.

As a result, it is entirely possible that the meaning of the monument—and the builders' purpose in creating it—changed from one century to the next. There is no guarantee that the people who carved images of axes and daggers into the stones knew why the Aubrey holes had been created hundreds of years earlier, for example. And the people responsible for digging the trench that surrounds the site may or may not have planned to set up the trilithons that form the center of the monument. Because none of the builders left any written records, the motivations, and in some cases the identities, of the builders remain difficult to grasp. "The Stonehenge we see today," writes archeologist Chris Scarre, "is . . . not the result of a single unified plan, pursued doggedly from century to century."[9]

Still, modern researchers have successfully determined the order in which the various features of the site were created. From the Sarsen

Ring to the Q and R holes, scientists have typically been able to date all the features to a range of dates no wider than a couple of centuries—and sometimes to ranges considerably less even than that. Most archeologists agree, for example, that the ditch that encircles the rest of the site was built within a period of just eighty years. But though scholars have this information, two important questions remain, both of them much more difficult to answer: who the various builders were and why they constructed the site at all.

Merlin and Magic

There has been no shortage of speculation over the years about who the original builders of the Stonehenge complex may have been. Today, some early explanations of Stonehenge's origins seem downright ridiculous. In the medieval era, for instance, it was widely believed that Stonehenge was originally built in large part by legendary creatures. In this story, popularized by Geoffrey of Monmouth in the 1100s, the slabs of stone used to make Stonehenge had originated in "the remotest confines of Africa"[10] and had been brought by giants to Ireland. There the giants quickly set up the Sarsen Ring and other stone features, which they used for healing purposes. According to Geoffrey, water that ran down the stones had the power to cure the sick. Why the complex needed to be built in Ireland rather than in Africa was a question that evidently did not interest Geoffrey.

The next step in Geoffrey's narrative was to explain how the stones came to England. Some years after the construction of the monument in Ireland, Geoffrey wrote, an English king named Aurelius Ambrosius wished to build a monument to commemorate a battle. He and his stonemasons, however, could not agree on a suitable design. Accordingly, Aurelius consulted with a wizard named Merlin, who in English legend went on to fame by advising the mythical King Arthur. Merlin told Aurelius to move the Stonehenge complex from Ireland to England and to set the

A fourteenth-century artist depicts the wizard Merlin tutoring Arthur, the young hero of legend. The cleric Geoffrey of Monmouth wrote that Merlin had a decisive role in Stonehenge being built in England.

stones at the battle site exactly as they had been positioned in Ireland. "If they [the stones] are placed in position round this site, in the way they are put up over there," Merlin supposedly told the king, "they will stand for ever."[11]

Aurelius, Geoffrey explained, did not have to be told twice. He sent his brother, Uther Pendragon (later renowned as King Arthur's father), to take the stones from the Irish. Unfortunately, though Pendragon's army easily defeated the Irish warriors, the stone monument proved too difficult for the soldiers to dismantle, even with ropes, ladders, and other tools. Amused, Merlin decided to intervene. He used his magic to take the stones down, place them on ships, and set them up at the Stonehenge site. Though Geoffrey did not concern himself especially with exactly when all this took place, it is clear from other evidence in his writings that Merlin's intervention would have occurred about 485 CE, or slightly over six hundred years before Geoffrey's time.

Romans and Druids

Other early theories sounded more promising on the surface but proved no more accurate than Geoffrey's hypothesis. In the 1500s, for instance, many people believed that Stonehenge had been built by the Romans. That notion certainly made more sense than did Geoffrey's tales of giants and magic. For one thing, Roman forces were known to have spent many years in Britain. Roman soldiers had invaded the island around 50 BCE, and by 50 CE Britain was essentially a colony of the Roman Empire, with much of Great Britain governed by and from Rome. The Romans, moreover, were known to be excellent engineers with a thorough grasp of technology; they had designed aqueducts, roads, and many other massive systems of public works. It made sense, from this perspective, to assume that the Romans were responsible for the monument. A bishop of the 1500s, for instance, insisted that "the stones were set up as trophies by the Romans."[12]

In the long run, though, this theory proved impossible to justify as well. There are in fact several strong arguments against a Roman origin for Stonehenge. The most obvious, perhaps, is the great contrast in artistry and craftsmanship between Stonehenge and the constructions in and around Rome. Compared to the Roman Pantheon, a temple built by the emperor Marcus Agrippa, or the Roman Colosseum, a large stadium now in ruins, Stonehenge is less sophisticated, less polished, and far less elegant. Still, many people did not see the differences or overlooked them in their desire to attribute Stonehenge to the Romans. That was true even of Inigo Jones, a widely respected architect of the 1600s, who was convinced that the Romans had built the monument. "How such a sophisticated man, who had seen the Colosseum for himself, could have thought that Stonehenge was an example of Roman architecture is something that has puzzled many people,"[13] writes author Rosemary Hill.

A third early theory of the origin of Stonehenge argued that it was the creation of a Celtic people known as the Druids. Unlike Merlin, the Druids actually existed; they were a pre-Christian religious group

THE PHOENICIANS

Over the years the origins of Stonehenge have been traced to an enormous variety of groups, including the Romans, the Druids, invaders from Denmark, and even the ancient Greeks. One theory that gained some traction in 1600s and 1700s tied the monument to a Middle Eastern people known as the Phoenicians. The Phoenicians, who were at their most powerful between about 1200 BCE and 550 BCE, occupied a long stretch of the coastline of the eastern Mediterranean Sea, near what are today Lebanon, Israel, and Syria. The Phoenicians were well known to educated Britons of the 1600s by virtue of their seafaring abilities and their trading experience. They had set up trade routes throughout the Mediterranean region and were believed to have sent ships as far north and west as England, in addition to possibly circumnavigating Africa or even visiting the New World.

The first influential writer to associate the Phoenicians with Stonehenge was probably a Briton named Aylett Sammes. The more Sammes thought about the Phoenicians, the more he admired them, and the more convinced he became that most of what was good about Great Britain was Phoenician in origin. That included Stonehenge. This theory was based on no evidence whatsoever, but many of Sammes's readers were nonetheless quick to champion his ideas. For several decades the Phoenician hypothesis was a common alternative to the more widely accepted theories that either the Romans or the Druids had been responsible for Stonehenge.

that flourished in England around the time of the Romans. As native Britons, the Druids were at first glance a reasonable choice to have built the complex. They were present on the island; they left no examples of more sophisticated architecture elsewhere; and to those curious about Stonehenge in the 1700s and early 1800s, they seemed far enough away in time to make their role in the building of the monument seem plausible. Since the Druids were a religious group, Stonehenge had in this view been built to serve a worship purpose—though whether as a church or in some other way was uncertain. Historian Joseph Strutt was one of many Britons who believed unreservedly in the Druidic origins of Stonehenge, which he referred to in 1787 as that "curious remaining proof of [the Druids'] indefatigable labours."[14]

Even the Druid theory had its flaws, however, but these were not apparent until more modern archeological methods came into being. Chief among these was a technique called radiocarbon dating, developed in the late 1940s by an American chemist named Willard Libby. This system measures the amount of a material called carbon-14 in once-living objects from antiquity, such as wood, bone, and charcoal. The older the object is, the less carbon-14 will be present, and the approximate age of the object can be worked out using mathematics. In 1950 Libby obtained a sample of material from the Stonehenge site and determined that it dated from at least 1500 BCE and was perhaps five hundred years older even than that. Since the Druids were not around at that time, it became clear to scholars that the Druids were not in fact involved in any of the Stonehenge construction.

The Neolithic People

In fact, more recent research has determined that 1500 BCE is much closer to the end of Stonehenge's construction than to its start. Modern scientists believe that the building of Stonehenge most likely began around 3000 BCE—long before the Romans, the Druids, or the mythical King Arthur. At the time, England—along with much of northwestern Europe—was going through an epoch in prehistory known as the Neolithic period. The Neolithic period was the last of

Druids perform religious rituals during an imagined ceremony at Stonehenge. Among the various theories of Stonehenge's origins is one that suggests the structure was built by the Druids as a place of worship.

three periods collectively referred to as the Stone Age, an era that spanned over 2 million years. The distinction between the three Stone Age periods pertains to the kinds of tools and weapons developed and used by the inhabitants of Britain and other parts of the world. As the Stone Age moved forward, the level of sophistication and effectiveness of weapons and tools evolved.

But there was an even greater distinction between the three periods. The Neolithic period represented a major change in socioeconomic lifestyle from the preceding Mesolithic period. The Mesolithic peoples of Britain had lived a nomadic life as hunters and gatherers of food. Small bands of people crisscrossed the land in search of deer and other game animals, staying only temporarily in any given place before moving on. As the Neolithic period dawned in England around 4000 BCE, however, the emphasis on hunting and gathering began to shift to a focus on agriculture and animal domestication. And as the peoples of Britain began spending more time growing crops and tending livestock than looking for food in the forests, they began settling permanently in places where the soil was good and the climate fair. The Neolithic shift, then, was to an agricultural lifestyle based on permanent or semipermanent villages and other small communities.

Because they traveled within a large area in pursuit of game, the people of the Mesolithic period had no special need to clear space for fields, build monuments, or otherwise leave a mark on their environment. There was little reason to put effort into such activities given that the game animals would soon move on, taking the group someplace else. Mesolithic Britons, then, built no temples, no farms, no meeting halls, and no enduring housing because they essentially had no need for them. A hut, a fence, perhaps a frame for a trap to catch a wild animal—these would have been reasonable objects for the people of the Mesolithic period to construct. More than that, though, would not have made sense to these nomadic people.

Once the Neolithic period began, however, things began to change. Since England was largely forested at the time, these Britons found it necessary to chop down trees in order to convert the forests to fields. That process, of course, changed the British landscape dramatically. The fields were used for growing crops but also as pasture for cattle, sheep, or other large domestic animals. Over time more and more wilderness disappeared, most of it leveled to feed an increasingly settled—and hungry—society. At the same time, people built larger and sturdier structures to house themselves, their animals, and their grain following the

harvest. They were no longer nomadic; they lived instead in a permanent location, and needed longer-lasting structures than their ancestors had required.

It took time, of course, for the Neolithic peoples of Britain to develop effective and efficient building techniques. As a result, few early Neolithic structures stand any longer. With the exception of an occasional barrow—a long earthen structure that often served as a tomb—most early Neolithic structures are known today only because of extensive archeological investigation. Scholars have found the outlines of small houses dating to the 3000s BCE, for example, even though no physical dwelling from the period survives. Nonetheless, it is fair to assume that as the people of Britain became more sedentary and more focused on agriculture, they became more adept at construction. By about 3000 BCE they had been building for multiple generations. Their techniques had been honed, and the Neolithic peoples of southern England were ready to tackle a large project such as Stonehenge.

The Windmill Hill Builders

The first parts of Stonehenge to be completed were the cursus, or "racetrack" just outside the main complex, and the outer ditch. The ditch has been dated quite precisely to between 3000 BCE and 2920 BCE. The builders are widely known as the Windmill Hill people; the name comes from another earthwork on a place called Windmill Hill, not far from Stonehenge. Not much is known about the specific features of Windmill Hill culture, but it is clear that the group fit squarely within Britain's Neolithic society. Technologically speaking, they were certainly capable of digging the enormous ditch that surrounds the monument; the evidence suggests that they were also expert makers of stone axes and other tools. Certainly they were a primarily agrarian society that grew wheat, kept cows and pigs, and built houses of wood.

Why the Windmill Hill people constructed the cursus and the ditch is unclear. Many archeologists believe that there were religious motivations behind the work, though exactly what spiritual purpose a circular trench might carry is not currently known. Others wonder if the ditch marked the outer limit of a marketplace or set aside a spot for the group's leaders to assemble and discuss policy. What is clear, however, is that the Windmill Hill people devoted thousands of hours to the project. In an agricultural society, time is usually limited

⬡ MODERN DRUIDS

In 1781, inspired in part by the theory that ancient Druids had constructed Stonehenge, a London man named Henry Hurle founded an organization called the Ancient Order of Druids. Hurle was intrigued by the attention being given to the Druids and decided that many of their principles were just as valid for late 1700s Britain as they had been back when the Druids had flourished. Other people soon joined his society, and similar groups began to spring up as well. Though these societies were set up largely along the lines of fraternal organizations, such as the Masons, there was a distinct religious flavor to them, too. As early as 1792 some Druids were holding worship services.

Interest in Druidism increased steadily through the nineteenth century and beyond. Today, about ten thousand Britons identify as Druids, and in 2010 the British government recognized Druidism as an official religion. The modern Druids, however, have had a tendency to disagree with one another and splinter into new organizations, many of them consisting of only a few dozen people. Author Rosemary Hill, in her book *Stonehenge*, mentions groups going by names such as the Order of Druids, the Reformed Order of Druids, the United Order of Druids, the British Druid Order, the Ancient Druids Universal Brethren, the Druid Order of the Universal Bond, and the Ancient and Archaeological Order of Druids, among many others—all of whom can in some way trace their lineage back to Henry Hurle.

as farming tasks can take all or most of the available day. Whatever the purposes of the trench and the cursus may have been, then, there is no question that they were of the utmost importance to the Windmill Hill people who constructed them.

One other feature of Stonehenge that belongs to the Windmill Hill people is the group of Aubrey holes. "It is thought that at first they held wooden posts,"[15] writes Hill, though this is conjecture at best and no one is entirely certain. At some point later on, though, the posts were removed—if they were ever there to begin with—and the emphasis shifted; the Aubrey holes were filled instead with cremated human remains and covered up. Again, why this change was made is unknown. This may well be an example of how the purpose of the monument changed from one generation to the next. The generation that dug the Aubrey holes had one purpose in mind, but a hundred years later that purpose had been forgotten, and a new generation had something else in mind. Archaeologists will never know for sure.

The Sarsens Arrive

The Windmill Hill people began the monument, but they did not finish it. Indeed, the stones that form the most recognizable parts of Stonehenge—the sarsen circles, the bluestones, the trilithons, and the miscellaneous slabs, such as the Heel Stone and the Station Stones—were not the creation of the Windmill Hill people. Rather, they were developed six or more centuries after the Aubrey holes, the cursus, and the outer trench—a period that roughly matches the distance between modern times and the Italian Renaissance of the 1400s.

While archeologists are generally agreed that the first phase of Stonehenge was created by the Windmill Hill people, there is less agreement regarding the identity of the people who set up the stones. Some archeologists argue that the raising of the stones was the work of a culture known as the Beaker people, named after the distinctive style of pottery containers they made. Where the Beaker people came from is a matter of debate, but they seem to have had an origin somewhere in continental Europe. By 2600 BCE some of them had migrated to Britain and settled in places such as Salisbury Plain, bringing along their distinctive forms of pottery and toolmaking, along with other customs.

In particular, the Beaker people were known for their ability to manufacture tools and weapons out of bronze—an alloy, or combination, of copper and tin. By modern standards these metal artifacts were quite rudimentary, but they represented a step up from the stone weapons and tools of the Windmill Hill people. For the next few hundred years, the people of England used both bronze and stone tools, and as archeologists define the eras, England began moving out of the

A distinctive bell–shaped beaker stamped with a geometric design is characteristic of the people known as the Beaker folk. Some archaeologists think that these people raised the stones that make up Stonehenge.

Stone Age and into a new period known as the Bronze Age.

The Beaker people did not arrive in sufficient numbers to take over the countryside by force. The best evidence suggests instead that they intermarried with the locals, changing the dominant culture over time by bringing in new ideas and materials. By approximately 2400 BCE, or so the theory goes, the Beaker culture was well established in southern Britain. According to this perspective, it was the Beaker people who began the process of setting up the stones at the Stonehenge site sometime between 2400 BCE and 2200 BCE, though these dates are less certain than the dates of the construction of the ditch and the Aubrey holes.

Completion of the Complex

Not all archeologists believe that the Beaker people were the ones responsible for erecting the stones, however—or at least, not for raising all of the stones. Some argue that the Beaker people may have brought the bluestones to the site, but that the work of gathering and setting up the heavier sarsen stones belongs to yet another early people sometimes known as the Battle Axe people. Like the Beaker folk, the Battle Axe culture was originally formed on the European continent, but some members of the group crossed the English Channel and settled in Britain at some point before 2500 BCE. As the name suggests, they were primarily warriors who did their best to conquer the peoples they came into contact with. Leon Stover and Bruce Kraig refer to the Battle Axe people as "a heroic, warrior-led society."[16]

Regardless of whether the shaping and lifting of the sarsens was the work of the Battle Axe folk or the Beaker people, the bringing and arranging of the stones was done by an entirely different group from those who began the monument. The same is true of the final phases of construction. Sometime between 2000 BCE and 1500 BCE another group, often known as people from the Wessex culture, set up a few more bluestones, shifted the locations of several others, and dug the Y and Z holes—though for whatever reason they seem never to have filled them with anything. The Wessex people, known as traders who brought a strong understanding of technology to their work,

WORDS IN CONTEXT
bronze
A metal formed from copper and tin.

were also most likely the ones who etched the carvings of daggers and axes into the monument.

Three different groups, then, and perhaps more, were primarily responsible for Stonehenge: the Windmill Hill people, the Beaker folk (and possibly the Battle Axe people as well) and the people of the Wessex society. These groups were related to one another only distantly by time and culture. There is no indication that the Windmill Hill vision of the site ever included the large trilithons, the standing stones, and the Y and Z holes that came along much later; indeed, there is no reason to believe that they intended any such construction. Similarly, it is likely that the outer ditch and the Sarsen Ring had a very different meaning and importance to the Wessex people than they did to the builders who preceded them. What is clear, however, is that there was never any single vision of what Stonehenge should look like—or of what it implied. It was, instead, the collaborative work of many generations, societies, and worldviews.

CHAPTER THREE

Construction

The construction of the Stonehenge site was a complex endeavor. The various people who built the monument had no modern tools. Not only did they lack power equipment such as bulldozers, but the tools they did have—hammers, axes, and so on—were quite primitive according to the standards of today. These tools had to be created by hand, whether from stone or from metal, and their effectiveness was limited. Despite these restrictions, however, the creators of the site did a remarkable job carving stones into curves, lifting lintels onto the tops of the uprights, and creating deep ditches and high embankments. "A stupendious [stupendous] Monument," wrote a traveler of the 1600s, who went on to marvel at "how so many . . . huge pillars of stone should have be[e]n brought together"[17] to create such an impressive site.

Exactly how the Stonehenge site was constructed is not well understood. The peoples responsible for building it left no written records. Neither did they leave models, diagrams, or blueprints. Through careful research, archeologists have been able to figure out some of the techniques used by the site's builders. However, many of the details regarding the monument's construction remain murky. In any case, the construction methods show a high degree of workmanship, a solid understanding of engineering principles, and a wealth of creativity. If nothing else, the fact that many parts of the monument have remained intact for several millennia speaks to the skill of the site's creators.

Creating the Holes

Of all the features of the Stonehenge site, the holes and small pits, such as the Aubrey holes, would probably have been the easiest to construct. While moving several cubic feet of soil can be a backbreaking task, it is certainly more straightforward than setting lintels on top of uprights or creating a nearly perfect circle made of stone. The holes of Stonehenge contain a number of deer antlers shaped into the form of picks, and modern archeologists generally accept that these were among the primary tools used by the Windmill Hill people to dig out the holes and trenches. There is evidence that some picks may have been shaped from wood, as well.

As far as modern experts can tell today, the procedure to creating the small pits went like this: First, builders used stone axes and other cutting devices to sharpen the antlers or pieces of wood, shaping them into tools that could easily loosen the chalky soil of the site. Repeated blows with an antler pick broke up the earth into clumps, which could then be removed from the pit with the shoulder blades of cattle—bones that are not only large enough to hold many pounds of earth but are also conveniently shovel-shaped. At that point the earth was dumped into baskets and carried away. Though the antler picks and the cattle bones seem primitive, they were more effective than it may appear. As a British history website puts it, "Modern experiments have shown that these tools were more than equal to the great task of earth digging and moving."[18]

The holes that served as supports for the sarsens and bluestones would have been somewhat more difficult to construct. Each pit would have been dug to a size that matched the size of the stone to be put inside it. That would have been a trickier process than digging the Aubrey holes or the Y and Z holes. It would certainly have involved some careful planning. As Chris Scarre writes, "The holes for the stones were dug to precise measurements for the lower ends of the uprights,

> **WORDS IN CONTEXT**
> friction
> *Heat resulting from the rubbing of surfaces against each other.*

Huge stone slabs intended for Stonehenge are transported with log rollers and manpower, as depicted by an artist. Experts say the methods used to build the structure demonstrate impressive workmanship and creativity as well as an understanding of engineering principles.

each one tailor-made for a snug fit."[19] How the builders made these measurements is unclear, but there is no question that the people who dug out the holes did a good enough job that many of the uprights remained in place for centuries.

A similar, though much lengthier, process would have been used to create the outer trench that surrounds the rest of the site. While any individual Aubrey hole could perhaps have been dug in a day or two of intensive labor, digging up the soil for the outer trench would have required thousands upon thousands of hours of work. Not only was the ditch close to 1,000 feet (305 m) long, after all; it was also 20 feet (6 m) wide and up to 7 feet (2 m) deep. Using picks made from antlers or wood would certainly have made the process faster, as would the use of bones for removing the earth from the trench. Still, the sheer amount of soil needing to be moved was overwhelming, and it is likely that the time needed for the process would have been measured in years. The one advantage the builders had in constructing the trench was in disposing of the earth; the soil dislodged from the trench was put to use in forming the embankment beside it, meaning it did not need to be carried far.

Moving the Sarsens

While the process of excavating Stonehenge's outer ditch required plenty of time, it did not require the level of knowledge and skill necessary to set up the stones. Indeed, the construction of the Sarsen Ring and the five trilithons inside the circle ranks among the most impressive feats of prehistory. To shape stones to specifications, lift them into place, and link them together—all the while measuring carefully to keep the stones level and evenly spaced—would have been an achievement even with modern tools, and it was a much more complex process without them. As with the digging of the Aubrey holes and the ditch that surrounds the site, there is much that experts today do not know about how the stones themselves were created and placed. Nonetheless, the broad outline of the project seems clear.

The first challenge would have been bringing the stones to the site. This would not have been in any sense a simple task. The sarsen stones weigh several tons apiece, and the Beaker or Battle Axe peoples had no engines to help with the process of moving them. And while the sarsen stones are not difficult to find in the southern part of England, they do not seem to appear naturally in the immediate region of Stonehenge. Certainly, as author Rodney Castleden puts it, "No one . . . seriously believes that the seventy-five new sarsens needed to build [the monument] were found lying on the ground near the site."[20] Most modern researchers believe, instead, that the sarsens were brought to Stonehenge from a place known today as the Marlborough Downs, located about 18 miles (29 km) from the monument site.

The most likely method of moving the sarsens would have involved platforms and ropes. By attaching ropes securely around a sarsen, it would have been possible for many laborers working together to pull one end of the rock off the ground. Through careful maneuvering, the sarsen could then be dropped onto a wooden platform. The platform, in turn, could be dragged over relatively level ground much as a sledge can be dragged over snow. Some experts believe that teams of workers did exactly that: They pulled the platform, together with its heavy load, overland to the Stonehenge site. Just how many workers would have been required to move a single sarsen stone, however, remains uncertain—and the speed at which they traveled is unknown as well.

⬢ CUTTING THE STONES

Today most archeologists believe that the great sarsens were cut largely by stone or metal tools such as axes and adzes. There are, however, other possible theories regarding how the stones were cut, and most scientists are not prepared to rule these out completely. Perhaps the best known of these theories involves fire.

According to this supposition, the builders first determined where they wanted to break a stone. Then they placed branches on that spot and set them on fire. The heat of the fire would weaken the rock. Next, the builders would abruptly pour cold water on the stone. If all went well, the temperature differential of the cool water against the heated rock would crack the stone exactly where the builders wanted to break it. The crack would probably not have broken the stone all the way through, but would have enabled the builders to use wedges and hammers to widen the crack and eventually separate one piece of the stone from the rest.

The builders may well have used this method from time to time. However, the technique is not very precise; there is no guarantee that the stone will crack at all when the water is poured onto it or that it will crack in the correct place. Since the builders had access to well-crafted tools, most researchers agree that axes, hammers, and adzes would most likely have been used in preference to the burning-branches technique.

Other Theories

Other researchers suggest instead that the builders used technology to help them, specifically by gathering logs to use as rollers. The platform would have been set on top of several logs laid horizontally. Then the arrangement gradually would have been rolled forward, with new logs being set into position in front of the platform as needed. The logs would have been coated in animal fat to provide lubricant and reduce friction, allowing the logs to roll more quickly and smoothly. As the grease wore away, the people in charge of moving the stone slabs would have replenished it as needed. Since much—though not all—of the land between the Marlborough Downs and Stonehenge is relatively flat, it is possible that rollers were used where the terrain sloped gradually or not at all and then abandoned when the land grew less even.

This process would certainly have been both difficult and time-consuming. However, moving the immense stones by ropes and rollers means would have been well within the realm of possibility. Into the 1800s similar methods were often used to transport large building materials. Indeed, there is pictorial evidence that they were used even in prehistoric times. As Christopher Chippindale writes, "The ancient Egyptians had shifted blocks of 800 tons"—sixteen times larger than the sarsens at Stonehenge. "Paintings in [Egyptian] tombs," Chippindale adds, "showed that they managed with the simplest gear. . . . It [is] clear that moving sarsens of 50 tons, or less, across the dry footing of the Wiltshire downland was not so difficult if you had enough hands, enough ropes, and a certain will and wit [intelligence]."[21]

There was one spot along the route, however, where the ingenuity and strength of Stonehenge's builders would have been challenged to their limits. That is a steep slope known today as Redhorn Hill. Here, it would have been necessary to lift the stones sharply upward and against the pull of gravity. The presence of the sarsens at Stonehenge most likely testifies to their ultimate success, but the amount of energy required to pull the stones up the slope would have been enormous. "Modern work studies estimate that at least 600 men would have been needed just to get each stone past this obstacle,"[22] a British

Bluestone from a Welsh quarry (pictured) is thought by some to be the source of rocks that make up Stonehenge's inner ring. Researchers have suggested various theories as to how the bluestone rocks were brought to the site.

website reports. Some experts argue that the slope was so steep, in fact, that it would have been virtually impossible to have moved the stones up that hill. In this view, the people in charge of transporting the sarsen slabs took a somewhat flatter but less direct route instead that would have avoided Redhorn Hill altogether.

Though most experts believe that human power was primarily used to move the sarsens to the Stonehenge site, some researchers argue that the builders made use of animal power instead. In this view, the builders harnessed oxen to the ropes and had them do much or all of the pulling. One study suggests that a team of oxen could have transported a typical sarsen stone from Marlborough Downs to Stonehenge in about two days. Moreover, since oxen are much stronger than humans, it might have been possible to move the stones with as few as one hundred animals, making the use of animals much more efficient than the use of people. Like many other aspects of Stonehenge's history, the truth will likely never be known.

Transporting the Bluestones

Moving the bluestones that make up the rest of the site's stone slabs was in one sense much easier than moving the sarsens; the sarsens, after all, were much heavier and bulkier than the bluestones. In another way, however, bringing the bluestones to the site was far more difficult than bringing in the sarsens. The reason is geography. Sarsen stones, though probably not available in the immediate vicinity of the Stonehenge monument, were common enough within two dozen miles or so of the site. The bluestones, however, were not to be found anywhere near the region. Geologically, the bluestone used at Stonehenge is closely related to a trove of dolerite found in southwestern Wales, nearly 250 miles (402 km) from the Stonehenge site.

For a time some researchers believed that the bluestone used at Stonehenge had been moved from Wales to southern England via glaciation. In this view, massive sheets of ice picked up the stones in Wales during an Ice Age and slowly but steadily brought them to England; when the ice sheets retreated, the slabs of dolerite remained behind. But while this theory is intriguing, it has its flaws. Since no other dolerite has been found in the area around Stonehenge, for example, the builders of the monument would have needed to find and use every scrap of bluestone brought over by the ice sheets. That seems unlikely. The only other explanation is that the people who built the monument brought the dolerite all the way from Wales—a distance more than ten times the distance needed to transport the sarsens.

> **WORDS IN CONTEXT**
> mauls
> *Hammers made of stone.*

Improbable as that may sound, it is the explanation preferred by most of the researchers who have studied the issue. Modern experts believe that the bluestones were moved in two ways: across the land, in a manner similar to how the sarsen stones were moved from the

◆ "ON RAISING AND FIXING THE STONES"

In the early 1800s a British author named James Easton put together a book he called *Conjectures on the Mysterious Monument of Ancient Age, Stonehenge, on Salisbury Plain*. It was a compendium of theories about Stonehenge and its origins dating back to Geoffrey of Monmouth and his Merlin-based hypothesis many centuries earlier. Though most of the book dealt with either descriptions of the site or the riddle of who had created the structure, one section—entitled "On Raising and Fixing the Stones"—took up the question of how the monument had been pieced together. The excerpt suggested that the builders of the site had first wrestled the uprights into place and then created "mounts of firm and solid earth for an inclined plane"— a sloping ramp, up which they could roll the pieces designated as lintels. When the lintels were level with the tops of the uprights, the builders set the lintels in place and then removed the earthen ramps. "There then appeared what we now call Stonehenge," the excerpt concluded. While modern archeologists generally support somewhat different theories about how the stones were put into place, the basic premise of "On Raising and Fixing the Stones" is sound and was a reasonable theory for the era.

James Easton, ed., *Conjectures on the Mysterious Monument of Ancient Art, Stonehenge, on Salisbury Plain*. Salisbury, UK: J. Easton, 1826, p. 78.

Marlborough Downs, and by sea. Most likely the stones were first dragged to the Welsh coast using rollers and ropes, then transferred to wooden rafts for the journey to England. According to this theory, the stones were next pulled up the River Avon to the general vicinity of Stonehenge, where they were brought overland to the site. Since the bluestones were smaller and more easily maneuverable than the sarsens, though, a few scholars have postulated that the builders used methods other than ropes and rollers to transport the bluestone slabs overland, including what one website describes as "supersized wicker baskets."[23] Like so much else about Stonehenge, we will probably never know the answer to this mystery.

The other mystery surrounding the bluestones, of course, is why the people who built the monument felt a need to go so far to get this particular type of stone. While dolerite does not appear naturally in the area around Stonehenge, many other varieties of rocks do, and it would seem reasonable to use one of them in constructing the site rather than venturing on a round trip of several hundred arduous miles to bring back these particular stones. There may have been some particular religious or spiritual significance to the bluestones; alternatively, undertaking such an extensive project may have been a way for the builders to demonstrate their wealth, power, and ingenuity to neighboring peoples, extending their influence over nearby groups or making the builders less likely to be attacked. Whatever the reason, there is little question today that the bluestones were brought to Stonehenge directly from Wales.

Shaping the Stones

Once the stones had arrived at the site, the next job was to shape the uprights and the lintels. Though most of the sarsens and many of the bluestones were already roughly rectangular, the builders needed to make them more uniform. In particular, they needed to make the uprights all more or less the same length and do the same with the stones destined to become lintels. Since the available technology did not permit joining smaller stones together to create a larger one, that meant cutting or trimming the larger stones to match the smaller ones.

For this purpose the builders of Stonehenge had only a few tools at their disposal. Mostly the builders seem to have used stone hammers, also called mauls, which consisted of a handle together with a rounded striking surface. The mauls were smashed repeatedly against the sarsens and bluestones, breaking off sections of the rock. Once the slabs were approximately the right size, workers used smaller stone or metal axes and cutting tools known as adzes to break off smaller chunks, shape the lintels into curves, and smooth the surfaces to the extent required. None of this was easy. Sarsen in particular is a very hard stone, and the work would have been both laborious and time-

The builders of Stonehenge probably used only a few simple tools to shape the stones. They might have broken off sections of sarsens or bluestones by smashing a maul, similar to the one shown here on the left, against the giant rocks.

consuming. To meet the builders' vision of the monument, though, doing the work would have been necessary.

There was one final step before the stones were put into place. To strengthen the rings, the builders used a complex system of interlocking pieces to join the lintels together. One end of each lintel was cut into a ridge, and the other end was notched. The notch and the ridge were the same size, allowing each ridge to fit neatly in the slot belonging to the lintel that would be placed beside it. This method, used today in carpentry more often than in stonework, is known as tongue-and-groove construction. In modern times, this type of construction is often used in making parts for toy roads and railroads, and the pieces of many jigsaw puzzles are created using a similar method. Again, mauls, axes, and adzes would have been used to create the ridges and slots.

A comparable design was used to attach the lintels to the standing stones. As Chippindale describes it, "Each upright bears on its top surface two conical projections, or 'tenons,' one for each of the two lintels it supports. Each end of each lintel has a corresponding hollow, or 'mortise,' which fits snugly over the tenon to hold it in place."[24] This tenon-and-mortise construction was probably not as sturdy as the joints that attached the lintels to one another; still, it showed an excellent understanding of engineering principles and an impressive degree of craftsmanship. As with the tongues and grooves that connected the lintels to one another, the tenons and mortises had to be fashioned using the hand tools at the builders' disposal. That was no small achievement.

Placing the Stones

When the uprights and lintels were deemed complete, it was time to wrestle them into place. Workers dragged each upright until one end was just over the opening of the hole. At this point the designers may have made use of enormous levers, probably made out of logs and branches, to push the stone up and slide it partway into the hole. Alternatively, the pushing may have been done entirely by people. In any case, the initial goal was to get the upright sitting in the hole at an angle. "Ropes were [then] attached to the top," a British website theorizes, "and teams of men pulled from the other side to raise it into full upright position."[25] If the soil around the upright was loose, laborers filled in any open spots with stones or dirt until the upright was solidly in position.

Once the uprights were in place, the lintels were next. The lintels had the advantage of being much lighter than the uprights, but of course they needed to be hoisted into a much higher position than the larger standing stones. As with many other aspects of Stonehenge, archeologists have several theories about how the lifting was accomplished. It is possible, for instance, that the builders made ramps out of earth and dragged the stones up to the top of the uprights. Another theory holds that workers used blocks of wood to lift the lintels. According to this theory, laborers lifted one end of each lintel slightly off the ground and placed wooden timbers beneath it, then did the same on the opposite side. The effect was to move the lintel slightly off the ground. By repeating the process dozens of times, the lintel would eventually reach the level of the uprights, from where it could be put neatly into place.

However it was accomplished, the building of Stonehenge was an enormous task. Castleden estimates that the work would have taken a total of 1.5 million hours, and others suggest a figure several times that amount. Digging the holes, moving the sarsens, bringing in the bluestones from Wales, shaping the stones, and lifting them into position would have been an astonishingly complex process—especially without wheels, pulleys, and other modern tools. The result, however, was impressive: a carefully planned monument that would last more than four millenia.

CHAPTER FOUR

Meaning and Purpose

Just as archeologists and other observers have had dozens of explanations over time of who built Stonehenge, from Merlin to the Beaker people and from the Druids to the Wessex culture, so too has there been no shortage of theories about why Stonehenge was built—and what its meaning was to the people who constructed and used it. As with the question of Stonehenge's builders, the theories about the monument's meaning range from the utterly implausible to the much more likely—and as time goes on and archeological methods become increasingly sophisticated, the theories have become ever more probable. Still, there is much researchers do not know about how Stonehenge was used and much they never will know about the value of Stonehenge to the peoples who lived there and constructed it.

Stadiums and Temples

Early ideas of the purpose of Stonehenge were many and varied. Those who favored a Roman origin for the site often argued that the monument was meant to be an imitation of the Roman Colosseum, which it very vaguely resembles. Some of these observers suggested that Stonehenge was a stadium of sorts, an enclosure in which people participated in games of different kinds. Indeed, the long road known today as the cursus—a Latin word meaning a racecourse—was given that name because of the widespread belief that it was used by Romans as a place for racing chariots, a common pastime in parts of the Roman Empire. Today, of course, evidence reveals that the cursus predates the Romans by several thousand years, making the chariot explanation impossible; but that information was not available to the British authors of the 1600s, 1700s, and 1800s who supported that argument.

Others who agreed that the Romans had built Stonehenge had a different interpretation of how the structure had been used. Inigo Jones, the English architect who studied Stonehenge in some detail during the 1600s, identified some similarities between the monument and Roman temples. Though most modern scholars attribute the similarities to wishful thinking on Jones's part rather than to any real connection, Jones used these supposed points of correspondence to argue that Stonehenge was intended to be a temple. In particular, he believed it was a temple to the Roman god Coelus, who was the god of the heavens—the original Roman god who gave rise to Jupiter, Minerva, Mercury, and all other Roman divinities. As Jones put it, Coelus was "the very Stem whence all those Deities in succeeding Ages proceeded."[26]

Another British architect, John Wood, had an equally dubious explanation of how the monument was used. Wood, who lived in the early 1700s, believed that Stonehenge was the creation of ancient Greeks who had settled in Britain before 100 BCE. In Wood's view, Stonehenge was essentially a map of the world. The site featured pits that marked the northernmost and southernmost extremes of the complex, and Wood convinced himself that these represented the "Artick and Antartick Circles."[27] Wood reported that the number of stones making up the monument had significance, as well. The thirty upright sarsens, for instance, stood for the thirty days of the typical month. In the end, Wood concluded, the site was indeed a temple, but a Greek one, not a Roman one, and in his opinion it was built to honor Artemis, the Greek goddess of the hunt.

WORDS IN CONTEXT
hypothesis
Theory that can be tested.

Over the centuries, many people have speculated on the purpose of Stonehenge. One theory held that it was intended to imitate the Roman Colosseum (pictured), which it vaguely resembles in terms of shape.

The Role of the Druids

Like Jones and Wood, those observers who believed that Stonehenge was the work of the Druids also favored a religious explanation for the site. John Aubrey, one of the first scholars to investigate the site and the man for whom the Aubrey holes were named, contended that Stonehenge and other somewhat similar monuments elsewhere in Britain were "Temples of the Druids."[28] Aubrey's interpretation was highly influential, and later commentators tried their best to determine how the structure might have been used as a temple. Some of the theories involved the use of human sacrifice, as evidenced by another name for a Stonehenge feature that has continued into the present day: the Slaughter Stone, widely believed at one point to have been used as a place where people—perhaps prisoners of war—were ritually killed.

Most of the early scholars who believed that the Druids had constructed Stonehenge, however, were not drawn to the notion of human sacrifice. They tended to be favorably disposed toward the Druids, seeing them as a gentle and wise people deeply in tune with nature, not as bloodthirsty warriors inclined toward murder, even for ritual purposes. This conclusion was based on little or no evidence. Few of the Druids' contemporaries wrote anything about them at all, and those who did had relatively little to say. In a sense, then, the Druids were a blank slate, and the people of the 1600s and beyond could interpret them however they chose. William Stukeley, a writer of the 1600s, was one example. In one of his works, he blithely stated that Druidism was "extremely like Christianity,"[29] even though Druidism began before the time of Jesus and flourished hundreds of miles from the Middle East.

Indeed, the people who championed the Druid theory interpreted practically everything about Stonehenge to support their position. To explain why the "temple" had no roof—a reasonable question given that most houses of worship in the 1600s and 1700s were covered—

one writer of the time theorized that Druidic burnt offerings to the gods made a roof unnecessary and indeed unwise. "The multitude and nature of their Sacrifices," this author writes, "requir'd such Fires as could not admit of [allow] Roof or Coverture."[30] Another writer argued similarly that the circular design of the stones was necessary for the Druids' own particular brand of magic. None of this could be proved, of course; but at the time, none of it could be disproved either, and many observers found arguments such as these to be compelling.

Still another commentator, a man named Hen Wansey, also believed that the Druids burned sacred objects on the Altar Stone, near the center of the monument. To check his hypothesis he made a trip to Stonehenge, where he burned various materials on the stone to see how easily they were consumed by flames. The answer, fortunately for those who liked the theory that Druids were responsible for the structure, was that materials burned quite well when placed on the stone and set afire. To Wansey and others who believed that Druids were responsible for the monument, this constituted clear

⬢ ALIEN VISITATIONS

Among the more bizarre theories regarding Stonehenge's purpose are ones that involve UFOs, or unidentified flying objects, and aliens from outer space. These theories vary somewhat from adherent to adherent, but they generally assume that Stonehenge was built in part or in whole by aliens and that the structure was originally intended for some extraterrestrial purpose. Swiss author Erich von Däniken, who believes that structures such as the Egyptian pyramids were created by civilizations from beyond our solar system, is probably the best known supporter of these hypotheses. Von Däniken argues that Stonehenge served as a landing pad for alien visitors eager to put their imprint on Earth.

Von Däniken is not alone. Several observers have reported unexpected lights and other strange phenomena in the skies over Stonehenge. While most experts have dismissed the lights as searchlights, nearby military maneuvers, or even the northern lights, a few who have seen them insist that the only possible explanation is visitors from other galaxies moving around in their spaceships.

The notion of UFO visitation is fundamentally based on two assumptions: a false belief that Neolithic Britons could never have constructed such a complex structure as Stonehenge, and the unproved and perhaps unprovable conviction that other civilizations have not only taken an interest in Earth but visited it, too. In the end, theories of UFOs are no more based on evidence than was Geoffrey of Monmouth's belief that Merlin was responsible for building Stonehenge.

proof that the Altar Stone was in fact intended for burnt offerings. Of course, the fact that materials did burn easily on the stone does not necessarily mean that the stone was actually used for burning, but Wansey had his theory, and he found the results of his experiments compelling.

Alignment of the Stones

Between the 1600s and the 1800s dozens of people presented theories about the use of Stonehenge. Most of these theories were wrong. Indeed, few were based on what modern researchers would consider evidence. To be fair, that was not entirely the fault of the theorizers, observers such as Jones, Wood, and Wansey. Scientific testing techniques that are taken for granted today were not yet available at the time. As a result, scholars had little opportunity to test their hypotheses in ways that could actually prove or disprove them. Nor did these men have as clear an understanding of history as scholars do today. To Wood, for example, it made perfect sense to imagine that the ancient Greeks might not only have paid a visit to Great Britain but might in addition have settled there. A more modern understanding of history makes it clear that the Greeks never took up residence on the island— but Wood could not have known that.

The people who studied Stonehenge between the 1600s and the 1800s did make one important observation, however, that turned out to be entirely accurate—and that seemed to strengthen the notion of the site as a temple. That was the alignment of the stones. The stones at the site are placed so that on the summer solstice, the longest day of the year, the sun appears to rise at one end of the stone circle and set at the other. According to an astronomy website, "If you stood inside the Stonehenge monument on the day of the summer solstice, you would see the sun rise above the famous Heel Stone."[31] Though the sun does not in fact rise *directly* over the Heel Stone, the variance is extremely slight, and most observers of the time agreed that the placement of the stones was intentional.

Further advancing the argument that the positioning of the stones

STONEHENGE AS SOUNDSCAPE

Recent research reveals that Stonehenge has some unusual properties related to sound. In the early 2000s a group of scientists studied the site's acoustics, or the way sound moves around the stones at the complex. They discovered that the site had acoustics very similar to those of a modern lecture hall; the sounds at Stonehenge would have been remarkably clear to listeners standing anywhere in the complex. "You could almost stand behind a stone and keep talking with a good level of voice," reports Bruno Fazenda, one of the researchers, "and people would be able to hear you somewhere else."

The people who constructed the stone circles may not have been aware of the arrangement's effect on sound when they set up the stones; indeed, Fazenda and his team suspect that they were not. And the builders may not have used the structure in ways that would have utilized this feature. However, Fazenda argues that the people who lived in the area around Stonehenge would surely have noticed that sound was not the same inside the structure as it was outside it. "They would have perceived [that] the sound environment around them had changed in some way," Fazenda reports. "They would say, 'This is different.'" It is conceivable that the sound qualities of the site made it an ideal spot for worship, drama, or some other activity that required people to listen closely to the words of someone else. Perhaps this was one of the main purposes of Stonehenge.

Quoted in Wynne Parry, "The Stones Speak," *LiveScience*, May 2, 2012. www.livescience.com.

was no coincidence is the fact that at the winter solstice, the shortest day of the year, the sun appears to set in the middle of a trilithon when viewed from the center of the monument. The most reasonable explanation for this suggests a religious observance, centering perhaps on sun worship. Though there was no particular evidence that the Druids had ever been sun worshippers, some influential writers assumed that they had been, and the notion stuck. For many observers, until the twentieth century, the main purpose of Stonehenge was assumed to be as a temple for sun-worshipping Druidic peoples. The available information seemed to fit the facts, and many of these scholars wanted to believe in the theory.

Gerald Hawkins

Through the late 1800s and into the beginning of the 1900s, the notion that Stonehenge was a temple of some sort remained quite strong, and the particular connection of Stonehenge with Druidism continued to be widely accepted. "Until the 1920s," writes Hill, "prehistoric monuments [in England] were marked as 'Druidic' on [official] maps."[32] At the same time, however, archeology was becoming recognized as a science, and by the early 1900s scholars were beginning to carry out excavations at Stonehenge that would look familiar to modern eyes. Between the late 1800s and the 1960s dozens of digs were performed at and around the site, each of them resulting in information that helped determine more and more clearly both when, and by whom, the monument was created.

In particular, those excavations eventually put an end to the notion that the Druids had been responsible for Stonehenge. All the available evidence indicated that the monument had been built many hundreds of years before Druidism even existed. And since part of the justification for calling Stonehenge a temple was its supposed connection to Druidism, scholars and other observers increasingly began to suggest that Stonehenge was not in fact a house of worship. What exactly it was, however, remained unclear—or at least it did until the 1960s, when an English astronomer named Gerald Hawkins announced that he had solved the mystery. Hawkins's theory discarded the notion that Stonehenge was a religious site and hearkened back instead to the discovery that the stones were aligned to emphasize the sun's rising and setting at the solstices. Stonehenge, Hawkins claimed, was an astronomical observatory.

Hawkins's theory, which he published in a book called *Stonehenge Decoded*, struck a chord among many of his readers. Hawkins had done extensive work on an early computer, plotting the locations of many of Stonehenge's most important features and comparing the locations to different positions of the sun and the moon. The results, Hawkins believed, were startling. "Not one of the most significant Stonehenge positions failed to line up with another to point to some unique sun or moon position,"[33] he wrote. In his eyes, this could not possibly be a coincidence. Rather, the locations of the stones and the other features of the monument had been carefully planned to emphasize—and keep track of—these alignments.

Other data, Hawkins noted, also seemed to point to the conclusion that Stonehenge was an observatory. There were fifty-six Aubrey holes, for instance, a number that matched the number of years between certain types of lunar eclipses. As Hawkins saw it, the holes were therefore a device for marking these lunar cycles for a society that lacked literacy. The entire complex, Hawkins explained, was a "Neolithic computer"[34]—a highly sophisticated way of following the

Although early scholars had little factual information about the Druids, many attributed Stonehenge to the workmanship of this ancient people (depicted). These scholars often concocted explanations to support their theories.

movements of the sun, moon, and stars. Despite living in prehistoric times with stone and metal tools, no system of writing, and at best a dim understanding of geography, the Neolithic builders of Stonehenge had developed a system of scanning the skies that would have impressed a twentieth century astronomer—or so Hawkins believed.

Debate

Stonehenge Decoded was popular with the public, and many readers accepted Hawkins's theory as accurate. Several other well-known scientists, on reviewing Hawkins's work, agreed. British astronomer Fred Hoyle, for instance, said it was virtually certain that the alignments Hawkins had noticed were intentional on the part of the builders. And Hawkins's ideas sparked similar theories from other scholars along with members of the general public. A museum curator in England, for instance, neatly fit several hypotheses together by arguing that Stonehenge had been built and used by a group of astronomer-priests in the Neolithic era and that Druidic groups descended from them had made use of the existing structures for their own purposes.

But not everyone acknowledged that Hawkins was correct. Many archeologists, in particular, found it impossible to believe that the Stone and Bronze Age people who constructed Stonehenge could have had such a refined understanding of astronomy. They argued that some of Hawkins's alignments were not truly alignments, with the sun or moon's actual position being as much as two or three degrees away from where Hawkins's computer model said it would be. Moreover, while they acknowledged that some of the most obvious connections between the heavens and Stonehenge's features were probably deliberate—the solstice sun rising almost directly over the Heel Stone, for example—they argued that most of these connections stemmed from coincidence, not intention. Theories like Hawkins's are "intriguing," writes Chris Scarre, "but simply don't stand up to careful scrutiny."[35]

WORDS IN CONTEXT

funerary
Having to do with burials or cremations.

The archeologists who opposed Hawkins have largely won this debate—but not entirely. The astronomers who subscribed to Hawkins's theories have successfully convinced most archeologists that the builders of Stonehenge did have the movements of the sun and the moon in mind as they made the monument. In particular, there is general agreement today that Stonehenge was designed at least in part to help its builders keep track of the calendar. Knowing when the solstice would arrive, for instance, would be valuable information for a predominantly agricultural society, one that needed to know when to plant, when to harvest, and how long to ration food in the winter. The question remains why the builders needed such an elaborate system of stones, holes, and other features to accomplish this goal, and most researchers have concluded that the calendar aspect of Stonehenge was by no means the only purpose of the site.

A Massive Cemetery

Most recently the scholarship regarding Stonehenge has focused on its use as a sacred spot—but not specifically as a place of worship. Rather, what strikes researchers today is the site's use as a cemetery. It has been known for years that human remains were present at the site and, in particular, that the long barrow near the monument was used as a place of burial. But until recently archeologists tended to downplay the notion that the primary purpose of Stonehenge was to serve as a graveyard. As a science website puts it, when archeologists of the early 1900s discovered bone fragments in their digging, they "thought the remains were unimportant and reburied them."[36]

In the later part of the twentieth century, though, that began to change. In 1978 a team of archeologists discovered a human skeleton in the outer trench at the site. Investigation revealed that the skeleton dated from the early 2000s BCE and determined that the skeleton had belonged to a young man who had been killed by arrows. On the theory that he had been an expert shooter himself, he was immediately dubbed the Stonehenge Archer. The discovery sparked a reevaluation of the importance of burials at the site. While no other skeleton quite like the Stonehenge Archer's has been discovered at the monument, archeologists have started looking at the site with new eyes, more prepared than their predecessors to consider the idea of Stonehenge as a burial place.

Indeed, the discoveries since 1978 have tended to confirm this theory. There are in fact many burial sites in and around the Stonehenge complex, some of them dating to the Stone Age, others to the Bronze Age. The barrow is the most obvious, but it is not alone. Several of the holes that dot the site, the Aubrey holes among them, once held cremated human bodies; some still do. Recent research on bone fragments and cremated remains suggests that burials go back to at least 3000 BCE, or the time that Stonehenge was begun. Other research indicates that the burials continued till 1500 BCE, the last time anyone did any work on Stonehenge, and likely beyond. Thus, Stonehenge was used as a burial site through its entire existence.

More Theories

The human remains at Stonehenge seem to come from a representative sample of the population. They include men and women, in roughly equal numbers, and some children. There is one important difference between the early remains and those dating from a later period, however. Relatively few people are known to have been buried at the site in its first five hundred or so years of use—perhaps as few as 250—up to 2400 BCE. This figure contrasts sharply with the much greater numbers known to have been buried at Stonehenge in the next several centuries. A number of archeologists have used this information to theorize that Stonehenge began as a burial place only for the builders' most important people—chieftains and their families—but over time became a cemetery for the masses instead.

In any case, the notion of Stonehenge as a burial site is increasingly well established among archeologists and other researchers. Mike Parker Pearson, one of the leading modern scientists to study Stonehenge, is one of many convinced that the funerary purpose of Stonehenge was paramount. "It seems to have been a cemetery all the way through,"[37] Parker Pearson argues. To be sure, its use as a burial site does not mean it did not have other possible purposes. There is evidence that at least some of the people who died at Stonehenge had been physically injured before they came to the site, suggesting to some researchers that the place may have been used for healing. And some experts have concluded that Stonehenge was used for ancestor worship, in which the bones and cremated remains of the dead were venerated and believed to be a part of the divine. These theories may prove to be true as well.

The meaning and function of Stonehenge have been in dispute for hundreds of years. Theories have abounded, including everything from a stadium to a burial site and from a massive calendar to a Druidic temple. Some of these theories have been based on significant evidence, while others have been based on virtually none. Today, in the early part of the twenty-first century, scientists seem to be making more and more careful guesses about what the value of Stonehenge may have been to the peoples who built it. Still, much of the mystery of Stonehenge persists; after all, theories have shifted in the past based on the discovery of new evidence, and the builders left no clear indication of their intentions. To some, this may not be such a bad thing. As Scarre writes, "It would be a sad day—and one happily still far distant—were Stonehenge ever to lose its mystique."[38]

CHAPTER FIVE

Stonehenge Today

As befits a monument on which construction began approximately five thousand years ago, Stonehenge is not in very good shape. Much of the damage took place, of course, long before the dawn of recorded history. By the medieval era, when Geoffrey of Monmouth postulated that Merlin was responsible for bringing the stones to the site, Stonehenge was already much diminished from its earlier grandeur. Even then, half or more of the structure's lintels and uprights were missing, with some of the remaining ones only marginally stable. Most of the holes that once dotted the site had been filled in, and the carvings on the stones had been worn away to such a degree that they were rarely visible under ordinary conditions. The centuries since Geoffrey wrote have been no kinder to the monument.

Over the years Stonehenge has been damaged in a variety of ways. Some of the damage has been the work of nature. Erosion from wind and rain, for instance, has made the carvings on the sarsen stones ever more difficult to see. Water pooling in the ground beside the uprights has weakened the structure. Rabbits and other animals have burrowed into holes used as grave sites, shifting bone and ash and making it difficult to tell what the holes were used for. Grass and weeds have grown over the causeways, making them hard to distinguish from the surrounding land. Silt and mud have filled in parts of the outer ditch. Though Stonehenge was well designed and well built, it has been unable to withstand five thousand years of damage from the natural world.

Harsh as nature has been to Stonehenge, though, the greatest dangers to the site over the years have come from another source: human beings. From the monument's very earliest days, people have altered the site in many ways. For reasons that are unclear today, for example, prehistoric peoples filled in the Aubrey holes soon after they were dug, changing how the monument looked and possibly altering the way in which it was used. Later, after the monument was complete, farmers planted and plowed fields that obscured the causeways and cursus and damaged the nearby barrow that held human remains. And while no one knows exactly what happened to the lintels and uprights that have disappeared, archeologists speculate that most were removed by people who broke them up for use in building homes or roadways. These massive blocks of stone may have fallen on their own, but they most certainly did not vanish from the site without help from humans.

Today, too, the greatest hazards to the well-being of Stonehenge come from human activity. The hundreds of thousands of people who visit Stonehenge each year have an impact on the site—and an impact that is almost exclusively negative. Military installations on the plain near the monument have caused damage to the structure, and to the holes, trenches, and earthworks that surround the stones. Cars, trucks, and buses passing the site on nearby highways bring pollution, vibrations, and noise, further endangering Stonehenge. Souvenir stores and other tourist-oriented businesses crowd the monument as well. Few of the great ancient sites in the world are at as much risk from humans as Stonehenge is today. How to keep Stonehenge accessible to visitors without risking further damage to it is the central dilemma of those charged with maintaining the site in the twenty-first century.

The goal for the custodians of Stonehenge—and for that matter the goal for the caretakers of most ancient structures—is preservation. That does not mean rebuilding the site as it might have appeared in 1500 BCE, let alone restoring it to look as it did when the Sarsen Circle was new. Instead, it means stabilizing the site as it currently appears and keeping it in reasonable condition so that future scien-

> **WORDS IN CONTEXT**
> erosion
> *The weathering of material due to wind and water.*

Hundreds of thousands of people of all ages and nationalities visit Stonehenge every year. The ancient structure is at risk from pollution, vibrations, and noise resulting from its popularity as a tourist destination.

tists may continue to study it and future tourists may appreciate it as visitors do today. Toward this end, the British government has dedicated public funds to pay for barriers, security personnel, and other expenses associated with keeping the monument undamaged. The government is to be commended for attempting to keep Stonehenge in its current form. How well these measures are working, however, is another question entirely.

Preservation

The desire to preserve Stonehenge dates back many years. As early as 1865 British author John Lubbock, noting the stresses on the monument from visitors, suggested that the British take steps to protect the site and keep it from being damaged. By modern standards, some intervention was clearly necessary. The monument was in private hands, so the British government had no authority over the site, and the owners—the Antrobus family—had little interest in hiring security officers to patrol the monument. Visitors, as a consequence, did not treat Stonehenge kindly. At best, they thought of it as an enormous picnic spot and playground; at worst, as a source of inexpensive souvenirs. Tourists "slid down the western trilithon until it was worn smooth,"[39] writes Rosemary Hill. They also carved their names in the stones, tried to push over uprights, left garbage from picnic lunches all over the site, and chiseled off pieces of the sarsens to remind themselves of their trek to see Stonehenge.

Scientists of the mid-1800s may have had more respectful motivations for visiting Stonehenge, but as Lubbock and some other observers saw it, their work also came close to ruining the monument. Eager to see what was below the stones, they dug rather haphazardly and without much attention to the effect their excavations were having on the uprights, and consequently made the massive sarsens more vulnerable than ever. The ditches and pits they dug disturbed the bones and ashes in the holes and made it impossible to tell how the remains were related to one another. And the methods they used to analyze the stones and estimate their age very often involved sledgehammers and chisels of their own. In the view of at least one member of the Antrobus family, Hill writes, "the experts were not always . . . much better than the outright hooligans."[40]

The rapid growth of villages and towns in the vicinity of Stonehenge, Lubbock believed, also threatened to overwhelm the site. The shifting of lands to agricultural use to feed a burgeoning population put extra stress on Stonehenge as farmers expanded their fields in the direction of the monument. With improvements in transportation, too, the number of people passing the monument each day rose, bringing an ever increasing number of residents into regular contact with the site. "As population increases and land grows more valuable," wrote Lubbock, referring not just to Stonehenge but to other British structures dating from ancient civilizations, "these ancient monuments become more and more liable to mutilation or destruction."[41]

The Problem Worsens

Distressed by the damage being done to the Stonehenge site, Lubbock tried to drum up support for transferring the monument to government control. He pointed out that Denmark was beginning to protect some of its own cultural heritage by buying up properties of historic interest. He also painted a grim picture of a land without its great monuments, a country in which Stonehenge had been reduced by scientists, tourists, and nearby townspeople alike to a shadow of what it had been even in 1865. But at first Lubbock's warnings received little attention. The notion that the government should buy private land was alien to most landowners and political leaders, and not many observers shared Lubbock's sense that the situation was rapidly becoming worse—or that Stonehenge might eventually cease to exist in even its mid-nineteenth-century condition.

Still, Lubbock did not back down from his position, and his writings did eventually strike a chord with the British public—and, more significantly, with some of Britain's more powerful people. In 1877 an organization known as the Society for the Protection of Ancient Buildings was formed. With the backing of some of Britain's leading thinkers, artists, and writers, the society helped persuade Parliament in 1895 to establish the National Trust, a quasi-governmental group charged with helping to preserve the cultural heritage of the United Kingdom. Armed with government approval and, more important, government money, the directors of the National Trust immediately set out to buy up some of the nation's greatest and most interesting sites. Stonehenge was on their list, but Sir Edmund Antrobus, who owned the monument at the time, refused to sell.

As the twentieth century dawned, matters quickly grew worse. Railroad lines sprang up alongside the site, bringing pollution and noise along with thousands of day-trippers eager to take home a slice from Stonehenge's great sarsens. Workers constructed a road, which soon became a highway, to meet the increasing popularity of cars. The road not only brought visitors but actually ran across a section of Stonehenge and came close to touching the Heel Stone. Britain's War Department commandeered hundreds of acres of land around the site for military maneuvers and training, causing the ground to shake and destabilizing the stones. And large numbers of tourists began gathering at Easter, the summer solstice, and other times throughout the

⬡ THE CRASH OF 1797

Through recorded history, very few stones have fallen at Stonehenge. On January 3, 1797, however, one of the remaining trilithons collapsed. The impact of this crash was extensive, as befit the weight of the stones. The impact could be both heard and felt 0.5 miles (0.8 km) from the site, perhaps further. The trilithon, which had already been tilted somewhat off center, fell onto its side and made an impression at least 7 inches (18 cm) deep in the soil. The probable reason for the crash had to do with the sudden thawing of ice and snow that had built up around the bottom of the uprights.

Those who had studied the monument before 1797 were naturally saddened by the crash. There were few enough stones remaining in position even before that January day, and now there were three fewer. "I could not contemplate without emotions of peculiar [special] awe and regret, such an assault of time and the elements on this venerable Structure," wrote one researcher of the time. But the disaster did help scholars answer a few questions, such as how deep the uprights had been steadied in the soil; and that helped to make up for any disappointment caused by the collapse of the trilithon. "These [negative] emotions were in some measure counterbalanced" by the opportunity to learn more about the site, the researcher admitted.

James Easton, ed., *Conjectures on the Mysterious Monument of Ancient Art, Stonehenge, on Salisbury Plain*. Salisbury, UK: J. Easton, 1826, pp. 72–73.

year to join together in worship, if they were so inclined, or in having a party, if they were not.

The Government Takes Charge

Growing increasingly worried about the damage being done, the Antrobus family cordoned off the stones with barbed wire around 1900 and began to charge admission. They also limited some of the activities that could be carried out on the grounds, most notably forbidding anyone to chip away pieces of the great stone slabs—though this rule was most likely broken on numerous occasions. No one much liked this solution, however. Visitors chafed at having to pay, the Antrobus family grew weary of trying to police the growing crowds, and an increasingly preservation-minded government worried that the owners might decide to tear down or otherwise alter Stonehenge past all recognition. In 1915 the property was sold to a man named Charles Chubb, who donated Stonehenge to the nation three years later. All over Britain people sighed with relief. Stonehenge, apparently, had been saved.

Certainly Chubb's gift helped safeguard the monument. The government was now free to carry out whatever policies it wished to protect and preserve Stonehenge without worrying that a private owner might act against the monument's best interests. Between 1918, when the British government acquired Stonehenge, and the dawning of the twenty-first century, Britain made a number of valiant efforts to protect Stonehenge. Some of these were highly successful. In 1927, for example, the National Trust was able to purchase some of the land surrounding the site, establishing a buffer zone between Stonehenge and the lands used by farmers and the military. Though the buffer was not fully operational until after World War II, the goal was a good one, and the measure has helped protect the monument into the present day.

Other actions have helped to preserve the site as well. Some of these originated with government. Admission rates were raised sharply in 1975, for example, which had the effect of limiting the number of visitors, thereby lightening the load on the site. The gov-

An eclectic mix of revelers, hippies, pagans, drummers and others make music and dance within Stonehenge's stone circle as they welcome the sunrise and celebrate the summer solstice. Celebrants often trample the land around the structure and leave behind huge amounts of trash.

ernment built a visitor center to explain the monument to tourists, too, which has helped keep people at a greater remove from the delicate structures and earthworks. Still other changes were the result of advances in technology. As archeological techniques improved, for instance, the scientific study of the site gradually caused less damage to the monument's stability and integrity. In addition, increasing the number of security personnel, which has been done from time to time, has helped to decrease the number of incidents of vandalism over the years.

The British government also received help and support from other sources during these years in its efforts to preserve Stonehenge. In the later part of the twentieth century, many countries began to take historic and cultural preservation more seriously than before. In particular, the United Nations formed an organization called UNESCO, in part to oversee historic preservation efforts. UNESCO has a list of properties it has designated as World Heritage Sites, a designation that qualifies the property for extra funding toward preservation, and Stonehenge—along with a nearby Neolithic site known as Avebury—joined the list in 1986. "These holy places," reads UNESCO's summary of the sites, "are an incomparable testimony to prehistoric times."[42]

Continuing Issues

But neither UNESCO's designation nor the various steps the British government has taken are sufficient to declare Stonehenge safe from harm—for now or in the future. The truth is that many problems remain. One of these involves the road that runs through part of the site. Many observers dislike the road for a variety of reasons. The constant traffic brings noise and pollution to the monument, which can damage the site; moreover, the road turns an experience that most believe should be undisturbed by the outside world into an experience all too easily disrupted. It is virtually impossible to stand in the area of the monument and not be aware of the heavy traffic along the roadway or how the road cuts off a corner of the site. In 1993 a government committee called the presence of a highway so close to Stonehenge "a national disgrace."[43]

How the site is used by visitors remains a significant issue as well. Much of the conflict today stems from a variety of groups that have patterned their religious worship after the Druids. Some of these neo-Druids continue to believe, all evidence to the contrary, that the original Druids built Stonehenge, while others, though recognizing that Druidism developed centuries after the monument was built, insist that the site was nonetheless central to Druidic worship. As the spiritual heirs to the Druids, these groups want unfettered access to Stonehenge in the twenty-first century. To date they have not gotten it, but as a compromise the monument is opened to any and all visitors on the summer solstice—a day

⬡ RECONSTRUCTION

Although efforts to maintain Stonehenge today are focused on preservation, that has not always been the case. In the past, several attempts have been made to repair damage and to restore the monument to look more as it once did. Some of these projects were carried out before the monument was in public hands. In the late 1800s, for instance, the Antrobus family hired workers to prop up some of the stones that were badly tilted. In 1901, with the Antrobus family still in charge, archeologist William Gowland went further by actually straightening a sarsen upright that was in danger of collapsing. To do this, Gowland's crew moved the stone 1.5 feet (0.5 m) to one side and encased the foot of the upright in concrete.

The drive to fix the structure continued into the period of government control as well. In 1958, for instance, concrete was added to the bases of three standing stones to help stabilize them. And in 1963, when one of the stones in the Sarsen Ring fell over, workers used heavy equipment to set it back into place and make sure it would not topple again. At the time, the decision was not controversial. Since the 1960s, however, scientific opinion on the subject of reconstruction has changed. If another stone were to fall, it is not at all clear that it would be raised back into place.

of special significance to the modern Druids. Unfortunately some of the visitors continue to expect a party atmosphere, and damage to the site occasionally takes place.

The tourist trade has presented other problems as well. Souvenir stores, restaurants, and other businesses sit very close to Stonehenge, as does the visitor center. Many people believe that, like the road, these establishments interfere with the experience of visiting Stonehenge. One leading English preservationist recently criticized the "clutter and rubbish"[44] that has grown around the monument. Again, for such an important cultural and historic icon, the notion that the grandeur and beauty of the site would be overshadowed by modern utilitarian architecture catering to tourists is distressing to many who love

Stonehenge. Indeed, UNESCO has expressed its displeasure with the current state of Stonehenge, mentioning especially the buildings that surround and constrain the site.

The Tunnel Solution

Unfortunately, finding solutions to these problems has proved politically and economically difficult. Some observers, for example, have suggested digging a tunnel under part of the site to reroute the highway that presently runs across one corner of Stonehenge. This idea, while sensible in many respects—it would conceal one of the main eyesores that currently mar the site—has met with significant resistance. Several opponents charge that the rerouting might cause further damage to the site underneath the ground, where other burial chambers or items of archeological interest may still be concealed. Others point to potential negative effects on owls, bats, and other wildlife. The Royal Society for the Protection of Birds, Britain's largest and most influential nonprofit nature organization, has come out against the proposed tunnel on this basis.

There are other worries, too. The price tag is one. Construction of a tunnel would cost millions upon millions of British pounds. In an era when the economy of Britain, like that of many other Western countries, is suffering, some argue that spending so much money on a project like this cannot be justified. Local residents worry that the project will serve mainly to make traffic worse. And even some supporters of the project acknowledge that a tunnel, while improving the looks of the site, will not actually do much to preserve and protect Stonehenge for future generations—which, many people believe, should be the primary goal of any work that is done in the area.

In 2013 a compromise was finally reached—one that did not satisfy all parties but was probably the best that could be achieved under the circumstances. Under this compromise, part of the road will be permanently closed beginning in the summer of 2014. In addition, a new visitor center is being built, and the existing parking lot has been closed with the intention of returning it to grass. The plan will

Under a 2013 compromise intended to protect the integrity and structure of Stonehenge, part of the road to the site will be permanently closed and an existing parking lot will be returned to grass. A new visitor center will also be built.

certainly eliminate one important source of pollution and noise along with improving the view visitors will have of the monument. "For the first time in centuries," says one official, "people will be able to experience this complex and extraordinary monument in a more tranquil, natural setting."[45]

Still, not everyone is happy with the result. One issue is that the new visitor center is well over a mile (1.6 km) from the monument itself. The stones, writes one disaffected newspaper reader, "will seem a distant matchstick model on the horizon."[46] Another is that the closing of the road does nothing to help solve traffic problems in the area; on the contrary, it will most likely worsen them, which may lead to anger and backlash from local residents and possibly from tourists as well. And the total projected cost of the project, while considerably less than the price of building a tunnel, is still quite high, leading to further criticism of the plan on financial grounds. Whether the road closure and the building of the new visitor center will help protect the monument—and whether it can be done at a reasonable price—remains to be seen.

Visitor Access

Issues regarding visitor access are not going to be easily settled, either. The summer solstice celebrations remain particularly controversial. Once boisterous (during the 1960s and 1970s they featured people clambering on the structure, spray-painting graffiti on the stones, and consuming enormous amounts of alcohol), they have been comparatively mild since the twenty-first century began. Still, that is no guarantee that this state of affairs will continue, and certainly the influx of thirty thousand or more tourists on a single day does not help keep the site in stable condition. On the other hand, tradition makes it difficult for officials to imagine shutting down the solstice celebration altogether.

The summer solstice is not the only debate regarding visitors, either. Some people would like to further reduce the number of visitors at the site in general. They point out that every visitor adds stress to the site simply by walking near the monument and that the infrastructure needed to support the arrival of hundreds of thousands of visitors—walkways, buses, a visitor center—puts further pressure on an already damaged Stonehenge. "What Stonehenge really needs," argues Christopher Chippindale, "is determined *discouragement* of visitors, not new facilities."[47] And vandalism, though fortunately rare in modern times, is impossible to police completely. In 2008, for instance, two people broke into the site after hours and used chisels to chip out a piece about the size of a small coin from the Heel Stone.

What the future holds for Stonehenge, then, is anyone's guess. Though most people agree that preserving the site as it is should be a priority, what that means is open to considerable debate. How much money should be spent on preservation; how acceptable it is to inconvenience tourists and local residents in order to keep Stonehenge as it is; and how—and whether—to mollify other interested parties, such as nature advocates: All of this presents a puzzle for the people in charge of Stonehenge today. Current and future generations can hope they make decisions that are in the best interests of the British nation as a whole—but particularly, perhaps, in the best interests of the monument itself.

SOURCE NOTES

Introduction: Stonehenge and the World Around It

1. Quoted in Rosemary Hill, *Stonehenge*. Cambridge, MA: Harvard University Press, 2008, p. 52.
2. Quoted in Brian Fagan, ed., *From Stonehenge to Samarkand: An Anthology of Archaeological Travel Writing*. New York: Oxford University Press, 2006, p. 20.
3. Quoted in James Easton, *Conjectures on the Mysterious Monument of Ancient Art, Stonehenge*. Salisbury, UK: J. Easton, 1826, p. 33.

Chapter One: The Site

4. David Keys, "Revealed: Early Bronze Age Carvings Suggest Stonehenge Was a Huge Prehistoric Art Gallery," *Independent* (UK), October 9, 2012. www.independent.co.uk.
5. Christopher Chippindale, *Stonehenge Complete*. Ithaca, NY: Cornell University Press, 1983, p. 15.
6. Leon E. Stover and Bruce Kraig, *Stonehenge: The Indo-European Heritage*. Chicago: Nelson-Hall, 1978, p. 85.
7. Chippindale, *Stonehenge Complete*, p. 15.
8. Hill, *Stonehenge*, p. 16.

Chapter Two: The Builders

9. Chris Scarre, *Exploring Prehistoric Europe*. New York: Oxford University Press, 1998, p. 131.
10. Quoted in David Roberts, "Romancing the Stones," *Smithsonian Magazine*, July 1, 2002. www.smithsonianmag.com.
11. Quoted in Chippindale, *Stonehenge Complete*, p. 22.
12. Quoted in Chippindale, *Stonehenge Complete*, p. 30.
13. Hill, *Stonehenge*, p. 61.
14. Quoted in Hill, *Stonehenge*, p. 49.

15. Hill, *Stonehenge*, p. 11.
16. Stover and Kraig, *Stonehenge: The Indo-European Heritage*, p. 65.

Chapter Three: Construction

17. John Evelyn, *Memoirs Illustrative of the Life and Writings of John Evelyn*. New York: G. P. Putnam & Sons, 1870, p. 233.
18. Britannia History, "Stonehenge." www.britannia.com.
19. Scarre, *Exploring Prehistoric Europe*, pp. 140–41.
20. Rodney Castleden, *The Making of Stonehenge*. London: Routledge, 2002, p. 146.
21. Chippindale, *Stonehenge Complete*, p. 131.
22. Britannia History, "Stonehenge."
23. History Channel, "Stonehenge." www.history.com.
24. Chippindale, *Stonehenge Complete*, p. 12.
25. Britannia History, "Stonehenge."

Chapter Four: Meaning and Purpose

26. Inigo Jones, *The Most Notable Antiquity of Great Britain*. London: D. Browne, 1725, p. 66.
27. Quoted in Chippindale, *Stonehenge Complete*, p. 94.
28. Quoted in Hill, *Stonehenge*, p. 33.
29. Quoted in David Boyd Haycock, *William Stukeley: Science, Religion, and Archaeology in Eighteenth-Century England*. Rochester, NY: Boydell, 2002, p. 167.
30. Quoted in Chippindale, *Stonehenge Complete*, p. 92.
31. EarthSky, "Gallery: The Summer Solstice As Seen from Stonehenge." earthsky.org.
32. Hill, *Stonehenge*, p. 130.
33. Quoted in Hill, *Stonehenge*, p. 168.
34. Quoted in Chippindale, *Stonehenge Complete*, p. 221.
35. Scarre, *Exploring Prehistoric Europe*, p. 142.
36. Stephanie Pappas, "5 Strange Theories About Stonehenge," *LiveScience*, March 12, 2013. www.livescience.com.
37. Quoted in Hill, *Stonehenge*, p. 202.
38. Scarre, *Exploring Prehistoric Europe*, p. 144.

Chapter Five: Stonehenge Today

39. Hill, *Stonehenge*, p. 142.

40. Hill, *Stonehenge*, p. 142.

41. Quoted in Hill, *Stonehenge*, p. 126.

42. UNESCO, "Stonehenge, Avebury, and Associated Sites." http://whc.unesco.org.

43. Quoted in Hill, *Stonehenge*, p. 167.

44. Quoted in Jill Lawless, "Ancient Stonehenge Gets Modern-Day Revamp," *Washington Times*, December 17, 2013. www.washingtontimes.com.

45. English Heritage, "Transformation of Stonehenge Landscape Begins with Road Closure," June 24, 2013. www.english-heritage.org.uk.

46. Robin Nonhebel, "Removing the Magic and Wonder of Stonehenge," *Telegraph* (UK), October 5, 2013. www.telegraph.co.uk.

47. Chippindale, *Stonehenge Complete*, p. 261.

FACTS ABOUT STONEHENGE

The Stone Circles
- The Sarsen Circle originally included thirty uprights and thirty lintels.
- Over 130 carvings have been found on the existing stones at Stonehenge.
- Most of the sarsen uprights weighed about 25 tons.
- Most of the sarsen lintels at the site measured about 10 or 11 feet in length (3 or 3.5 m).
- The Sarsen Circle has a diameter of about 108 feet (33 m).
- The inner bluestone ring is about 75 feet (23 m) in diameter.

Other Stones
- The Altar Stone is about 16 feet (5 m) long.
- There were originally two pairs of Station Stones at the site, but just one of each pair survives.
- The Slaughter Stone measures about 7 feet (2 m) wide.
- The tallest upright sarsen in the horseshoe figure measured 24 feet (7 m) in height.

Ditches and Causeways
- The outer ditch of the complex measures 330 feet (100 m) in diameter.
- The width of the outer ditch at Stonehenge is about 20 feet (6 m).
- The Avenue, or main causeway, is about 35 feet (11 m) wide.
- The Stonehenge Cursus was about 1.8 miles (3 km) long.

Holes
- There are fifty-six Aubrey holes at the site.
- Most Aubrey holes had a depth of about 2 feet (0.61 m).
- The site included about forty each of the Q and R holes.

Stonehenge Today

- About half the Aubrey holes have been excavated; the others remain largely filled in.
- Three complete trilithons are currently standing; parts of the other two have fallen.
- The Altar Stone is mainly concealed beneath the fallen stones of one trilithon.
- The Heel Stone currently leans at an angle of about 27 degrees away from vertical.

FOR FURTHER RESEARCH

Books

Marc Aronson, *If Stones Could Speak*. New York: National Geographic, 2010.

Christopher Chippindale, *Stonehenge Complete*, 4th ed. London: Thames and Hudson, 2012.

James O. Davies, *A Year at Stonehenge*. London: Frances Lincoln, 2013.

Jesse Harasta, *Stonehenge: History's Greatest Mysteries*. Boston: Charles River Editors, 2013.

Rosemary Hill, *Stonehenge*. Cambridge, MA: Harvard University, 2008.

Michael Parker Pearson, *Stonehenge: A New Understanding*. New York: Experiment, 2013.

Websites

Britannia History, Stonehenge (www.britannia.com/history/h7.html). Includes pictures and text regarding Stonehenge, its construction, and its possible uses.

English Heritage, Stonehenge (www.english-heritage.org.uk/days out/properties/stonehenge). An official site of the Stonehenge monument, providing information about visits and history.

History Channel, Stonehenge (www.history.com/topics/british-history/stonehenge.) A description of Stonehenge together with information that is known about it. Includes photos and links.

NOVA, Stonehenge: Expert Q&A (www.pbs.org/wgbh/nova/ancient/stonehenge-questions.html). A question-and-answer interview with archeologist Julian Richards, who has studied Stonehenge extensively.

UNESCO, Stonehenge, Avebury, and Associated Sites (http://whc.unesco.org/en/list/373). UNESCO's description of Stonehenge and an explanation of its historic and cultural value.

INDEX

Note: Boldface page numbers indicate illustrations.

and popularity of site, 13, 67, 68, 71–72, 73
traffic issues, 70–71, 74, 76–78, 77
trenches. *See* ditches
trilithons
  construction of, 43
  crash of 1797 of, 71
  and damage from tourists, 69
  described, 17
  winter solstice and, 59

UFOs, 57
UNESCO, 73–74
Uther Pendragon, 11, 28–29

utilitarian, defined, 74

vandalism, 78

Wales, 47–49
Wansey, Hen, 56–67, 58
Wessex people, 38–39
Windmill Hill people, 34–36, 41
winter solstice, 59
Wood, John, 54
Wordsworth, William, 18
World Heritage Sites, 74

Y and Z holes, 23, 38

PICTURE CREDITS

Left: hand hammer (stirrup maul)/Werner Forman Archive/The
Bridgeman Art Library: 50

Stonehenge (gouache on paper), English School, (20th century)/
Private Collection/© Look and Learn/The Bridgeman Art
Library: 61

ABOUT THE AUTHOR

Stephen Currie has published dozens of books and other educational materials. His works for ReferencePoint Press include *The Medieval Castle*, *Goblins*, and *The Future of Hydropower*. He has taught at levels ranging from kindergarten to college. He lives in New York State.